This book by Audrey hope to many who need freedom and wholeness in their lives. Audrey has a wonderful gift of evangelism and healing that comes across clearly throughout this book. If the Son sets you free, you are free indeed.

Pastor Ed Hird

I had the privilege of reading through Audrey Mabley's book. It has been an invigorating read. Her life is a reflection of what God can do through a committed, repented vessel. It is my prayer that as you read through the pages of this autobiography, you will not only be blessed but also inspired to be all that the Father has intended for you to be. Read, digest, then go forth and do the Will of God! Thanks, Audrey.

Michael Scantlebury-Apostle
Dominion–Life International Ministries
www.dominion-life.org

I am pleased to be able to give my support as Mayor of Burnaby to the Eternity Club founded by the Reverend Audrey Mabley.

We are fortunate to have a club such as the Eternity Club, which dedicates itself to providing support to those who need it.

William J. Copeland
Former Mayor of Burnaby, BC, Canada

It is my pleasure to recommend the work of the Eternity Club Ministry. Having attended their anniversary celebrations over the past years and hearing the firsthand personal testimonies, I could see the good work this club is doing.

The Eternity Club hosts many programs (feeding programs, prayer and counselling, a caring church, and radio program). The club is a friendly caring ministry. Their founder claims people need to know they're loved by God and that someone cares

Fred Randall
Former MLA, Burnaby- Edmonds, BC, Canada

Rev. Audrey Mabley has faithfully served as a pastor of the Lord's people locally and especially as an effective evangelist to the wider community. She is deeply grounded in prayer and seeks to minister *with signs following*. Audrey has established a track record of honesty, integrity and sensitivity to the Lord from which she ministers *as of the ability God gives*.

Lionel C. Batke, President
Release Ministries Society

Audrey exemplifies what is meant by 'It is no longer I who live, but Christ who lives in me." She exudes love for others and passion for all to come to know the loving embrace of Jesus. To be around Audrey is to sense the peace of Christ, which is actually amazing given that she shows no signs of slowing down in her ministry, but it is not that kind of peace.

It is in her unshakable faith in the Lord that one senses the peace, and that just seems to give her strength for the day, for trials, for ministry, for family and for any of us who just need a prayer and a moment.

Steve Almond
The Light Magazine
604-510-5070 ext 105
www.lightmagazine.ca

When Audrey heard three words "God loves you" from a female pastor, it planted a seed that dramatically changed her life. This hard drinking woman became a top evangelist. Through her radio and television shows directly, inside or outside church walls, many tens of thousands have heard Audrey repeat these same words. We will never know this side of heaven just how many people this has affected.

Anyone can count the seeds in an apple but no one can tell you how many apples are in a seed. This book will plant many more seeds.

It has been a honor to be part of Audrey's team for over a decade.

Stuart Spani
Founder, Norlynn Audio Visual Services

THANK GOD

I MARRIED AN

ALCOHOLIC

An Autobiography

REV. AUDREY MABLEY

ISBN: 978-1-4866-0504-0

Word Alive Press
131 Cordite Road, Winnipeg, MB R3W 1S1
www.wordalivepress.ca

WORD ALIVE
—P R E S S—

Cataloguing in Publication may be obtained through Library and Archives Canada

CONTENTS

ACKNOWLEDGEMENTS

I would like to thank Garrett Golhof for his strong encouragement to write this book and Shirley & John Svoboda that helped make it possible!

Also Barbara Hill for the hours of labor editing and going over it to make it the best we could! Thank you, Barbara for your patience! My husband and family for their kindness in the process it took to finally get it to print ! Most important, my Heavenly Father that enabled me to have a good story to tell ... AMEN !

A NOTE FROM THE AUTHOR

As you hold this book in your hand, it is my prayer that Father God would grant you a revelation of His love for you. This true story makes very clear how God can change, heal, and bless in awesome ways as we yield to Him through Christ our Lord. No matter what you've been through, or what is in your past, or how weak you feel, God can do mighty things in your life.

Enjoy reading what God has done!
In Christ's Name & Love
Rev. Audrey Mabley

CHAPTER **1**

IN THE
BEGINNING

MY EARLIEST MEMORIES ARE FROM WHEN I WAS SIX YEARS OLD and living in Webster's Corners, seven miles from Haney, British Columbia, Canada. We lived about three miles from the closest store and school, which were located at an intersection called Webster's Corners. Down the main road was a community hall, and Dad told me that when I was twelve years old I could go to a dance there. The thought of that excited me.

My father was very young when he married my mother. He had just turned sixteen, and my mother was nineteen. When I was seven, Dad was only twenty four years old. I remember being very proud of my good looking father. He had a wonderful singing voice, his own band, and could play guitar, violin, and even piano all by ear. He was very talented.

There were good times in the old two story farm house. On the main floor we could go around in a complete circle. Dad used to play "Choo-choo train" with us. We would all line up one behind each other and go around the house in a complete circle saying, "Choo-choo, Chug-chug." It was such fun.

Our country home was on eighty acres of land at the foot of a mountain. I can remember the old washing machine

Audrey at 7 years old, 1945 (first girl in second row).

Mother had. It had a large handle that came out from the side. Mama or one of us kids would pull the handle out and in, and this caused the agitator inside the tub to move and clean the clothes. We could connect the old rocking chair to this handle and be amused that clothes could be washed while we rocked.

There was a creek that ran down from the mountains about half a block from our house. We used buckets to get our water from this creek. It was not uncommon to find small trout in our drinking dipper. This never seemed to bother us. We all drank from the same dipper. It was like a tin cup with a long handle and sat all day in the water pail.

I think of our dear mama carrying water to wash clothes. Mama was in her twenties and five feet tall. She weighed ninety-eight pounds and had red hair like me. She worked so hard for the family that she developed a hernia the size of an egg. I felt sorry for her. I used to tell her that when I grew up and got rich I was going to buy her lots of beautiful

Audrey's dad Maurice Dame, 24 years old, 1948

things. I didn't have to do that, because when I was thirteen Dad left Mom and she eventually married a good man named Len Wallace, and he left her well taken care of—thank God.

I also remember that when I was about seven, some farm boys that lived next door put a handful of live worms down my back. I ran home screaming, so petrified that my mother could not make head or tail of what was wrong with me. I kept pointing to my back and screaming. Finally, she freed me from this terror.

There were five girls and one boy in our family at this time. In the summer, my sisters and I used to sit on the back porch of the old farm house and eat peanut butter by the spoonfuls, and at other times we would eat rhubarb dipped in salt we had shaken into our palms.

I well remember we had one cow, so we always had fresh milk. Dad was the milker, but we had fun trying. I was only around six years old when we had two baby pigs. They were so small and cute, and it was my chore to feed them. They

Grandma Sider, mom Lillian, sisters Baby Linda,
Uncle Fred, Carole, Audrey, & Marion, 1950

loved me and even followed me to school, which was about a mile and a half away. That caused quite a stir. However, the pigs grew big and Dad said it was time to take them to the slaughter house. I was so upset—and then they wanted me to eat the meat. I sat at the kitchen table with a sad face and refused to eat.

One winter Grandpa Pete Dame, my dad's father, made a sleigh with a couple of logs and planks across. He nailed some wooden chairs on the sleigh, hooked up Kingo, Dad's work horse, and drove us to school. The kids were so envious. That was such a happy time. I'm so grateful I had some good times when I was young.

Our neighbours, the Debots, had a very large natural swimming pond that had clear water, and people could swim in it. They owned the property, and we wished we had a pool like they did. One noble thing Dad attempted to do was dig us a swimming pool. He dug an area around our property about fifty feet round. He was about twenty-two years old at that time and very strong. After he was done he hooked up a hose from the house and filled it with water. We were so excited; we thought we had our own private swimming pool. However, we were very disappointed because it was just a mud hole. I think he got drunk after that, as he made homemade beer that was always handy.

My dad's brother, Uncle Tommy Dame, came to visit us. He weighed about three hundred pounds. We rarely used the front door of our house, and unknown to us, each step was rickety. One day when he tried to enter the house through that door, each step he took broke the stair under his weight. About the third step, he gave up and came in the back door. They never did get fixed.

It was not uncommon for us girls to be upstairs in bed while Daddy had a country hoedown downstairs with lively country music playing. Dad would be playing guitar with a harmonica hooked up to his mouth. Grandpa would be on the fiddle. This happy music would filter upstairs and be so grand to fall asleep with. Therefore, to this day, my favourite music is country.

When Dad did exceptionally well at his shingle-shake business on our land, our Christmases were tremendous. One I will never forget was when Dad, an artist at tree decorating, outdid himself by decorating the tree superbly with lights shaped like candles that bubbled. There were so many gifts— dolls for us girls, and even doll buggies and little high chairs. We were so happy and thrilled to have so much from Santa.

While living in the old farm house in Haney, my sister Carole and I had to walk approximately three miles to the country school house. The kids would bump us on purpose and then say, "Ew, fleas. Don't go near them." It felt horrid and increased the feeling I already had of being unwanted and unloved, especially by my father. I believed he loved my sister Carole more, because she never got punished for anything. If Mother ever thought of disciplining her, Carole would firmly declare, "If you touch me, I'll tell Dad."

As I reflect on why the kids were so mean to us, I think it was because of our own father's activities of drinking and running around, and they heard their parents talking about him negatively. As I mentioned, my self esteem was very low. I believed that I was ugly. There was an extra tooth between my two front teeth that looked like a v-shaped fang. I stood in front of my mother's dresser mirror and told myself that I looked like a witch. I had poker straight, flaming red hair. My mom tried to make me look better by braiding my hair at times, but even before I got to school they would come undone. In contrast, my sister Carole had beautiful, curly hair. I thought she was so beautiful, and I was like an ugly duckling. Maureen (Marie), my sister one year younger, also was pretty with curly hair, too.

My dear mother loved me all she could or dared, for I believe she was afraid of my dad. I was terrified of Dad and his brown eyes that seemed to radiate to me fear and anger. He would yell at Mom and say, "Do what I say, Lil, or you will be six feet under." I believed he meant it, and I think Mom did, too. Sometimes at the supper table, Dad would go one by one and call us by name and ask, "Who do you love the most?" All the kids said "Daddy," and I said it, too, being afraid to say "Mama," but in my heart I said "Mama." When I was born, mother weighted sixty-nine pounds. She told me she had not eaten for three days. I now believe I came into this world hungry. Mom's normal weight was usually ninety-eight pounds.

My mother was very loving, and because of this I knew there was love in the world. She was kind, soft spoken, and

Audrey at 13, 1951

kept the house spotless. She'd bake bread (so good, hot, and fresh), make pastries, and prepare good meals (when we had the money). During the depression, there were times we were very, very poor, and often ate bannock. That is what you make when you don't have enough ingredients for pancakes.

Mama told me that when Carole and I were both babies (we were born a year apart), we needed milk and there was none. Mom went to the corner store to ask for a quart of milk for her babies and was told by the man at the store that he would give her a quart of milk for "privileges." This was very traumatic for our mom. She must have thought, "My babies will starve." It's no wonder that she began to cry and bang her fists against the apartment wall, yelling, "Someone help me." Meanwhile, Dad was out likely partying with a friend. The neighbours came in and Mother received some help. This happened during the depression days. The government gave struggling families food stamps, but I think Dad sold them and bought alcohol.

In grade three, when I was eight, I stole a nickel. When Dad found out, I knew I was going to be punished. He took out a razor strap for me to see. This razor strap was a piece of leather. He proceeded to put salt, pepper, and vinegar on it. While I was watching my dad, he explained that this was to make the razor strap hurt more. Then he turned me over his knee and he whipped me with the strap. He beat me to semi-consciousness. I can still remember my mother yelling and pleading in a loud voice, "Morry, STOP. You will kill her." He finally did stop. I knew he was sorry, because he took me and Carole to a movie that same night; however, I could barely sit down. One thing is sure—I never stole again.

I often wondered if maybe Dad loved Carole more than me because she was so pretty and I was not. She could even sing better than I could. Carole and Maureen would gather around Dad while he played his guitar. Dad would play the guitar and sing merrily along with the girls. I felt so very left out. He would say to me, "Audrey, go in the kitchen. Go see your mother."

Mother tried to compensate for the way Dad treated me, so that at times I would feel like I was her favourite. When I was about eight, due to family pressure, especially from my dear Aunt Tilly (my dad's sister), things changed and everything Carole received, I received, too. This was heaven to me.

I was an unusual child and would not fight back. When my sister would kick my shins on the way home from school, I would not strike back. Mother would ask me why I did not fight back. I really had no answer for her. My logic seemed to be that if I was hit and I hit back, a real fight would commence. However, if I did nothing, the instigator would soon be bored with a one-sided fight and there would be peace. This is how I reasoned at this early age.

When we left Webster's Corners, I rode with Carole on the back of a large flat deck truck with no sides. It was scary, because I knew if I let go, I would surely fall off and die. It was all so exciting with the wind blowing in our faces as the truck went fast.

We were on our way to Winnipeg, Manitoba. Compared to B.C., it sure was cold there in the winter. Mom would go out with a kettle of water to prime the community water pump down the street, because overnight the pipe would freeze. The hot water thawed the pipes, so she could get water to our home. Imagine hauling water half a block for laundry, etc. Snow drifts were six feet high. Our bedroom windows had snow almost to the roof, and we had to use lights in the daytime because the window had snow blocking our daytime light. We never saw daylight in our bedrooms until the spring thaw.

We went to a Catholic school, and a van picked us up daily. Many years later in my life, a sister in the Lord named Avis, secretary at the *100 Huntley Street* Vancouver office, told me a beautiful older day parable to do with pumping water from an old fashioned pump. The first water pumped is gucky, but as you persist it gets clearer and clearer. So it is in our walk with God, our Lord Jesus. At first it is a bit rough, even rocky, then things smooth our more and more as we walk with God.

In this home at age ten, I built a small altar and put a candle on it and a soft cloth. I would kneel and pray with tears streaming down my face. My mother told me this when I was forty-two. I had forgotten the event, but she reminded me about it. I can see clearly, now, that even at this early age God was drawing me near to Him.

We moved back to Vancouver, British Columbia, when I was ten years old. The Salvation Army came around with a band and played on our street corner on Second Avenue near Henry Hudson School. Their songs delighted me. We sang, "Jesus Loves Me," and "My cup is full and running over; since the Lord saved me I am as happy as can be ... my cup is full and running over." This was in 1947, and very soon I came close to death.

My appendix ruptured. A neighbour came over and Mother called a doctor. I knew I was dying, and I felt like I was falling. I was very cold. Mother said my skin was blue. Mom and our neighbour began to massage my body; everywhere they rubbed, I felt life returning. I yelled, "Oh, God, help me. Save me!" Then I would yell, "Rub harder, everyone. Please!" They did. The doctor came and I was rushed to St. Paul's Hospital for emergency surgery. The Sisters there told Mom that I had only a fifty-fifty chance to survive, so they gave me the Catholic last rites, just in case. Thank God I am alive and writing.

Dad organized a band in which he sang. As I mentioned before, he had such a lovely singing voice. Carole and I would go door to door selling tickets to Dad's dances. We were now about twelve and very proud of our singing father. We were living in Burnaby, B.C., and Dad built a house near Sprott Street.

In my younger years, I was close to God (always saying my prayers). I would try to get Carole to say hers. In later years, she confided in me that she would tell me to leave her alone as though she was angry at me, then she would go ahead and say her prayers, too. It was rare for me to misbehave. My desire was to be a good girl at home and at school. I loved any praise at all.

When I was thirteen, Mom and Dad separated. I understand he treated his second wife like he treated my mom. By this time I discovered I wasn't ugly, and if I stayed out of the

Audrey at 14 & Cousin Anita, 15

sun, I wouldn't get the big freckles. If I pin curled my hair (which I did), my hair looked nice. When I was twelve, I was not afraid to smile anymore because my mother took me to a dentist and he removed my "fang." We were living on 8th Avenue in Vancouver, and I'd met a Danish fellow named Anthony who had a car. He told me his car backed up ten feet for brunettes, twenty feet for blondes, and fifty feet for red heads. That made me feel special.

When we moved from there to Chester Street near Marine Drive, I met Patrick Kinzie. I had to sit on Pat's knee in the moving van, and I was very shy. I was also very hungry for love, especially from a man. Pat adored me and called me his "Angel," and he bought me pretty clothes. I was an innocent lamb heading for the trials of life.

Patrick was twenty-one years old, and I was only thirteen and a half. I loved him so very much. He was kind, considerate, and a gentleman interested in me in a way that I never had experienced before. He even went so far as to ask

Patrick & Audrey Kinzie, March 20, 1954

me what I had been eating. He would take me out for nourishing meals, and I tasted my very first veal cutlet with him. We rarely had much nourishing food at home. I don't recall eating fruit as a child, and I drank very little milk, as the milk in the house was always for the baby in our large family. There always seemed to be a baby with needs in our family. Mom eventually had eight kids—seven girls and one boy.

After Pat and I married, it felt so awesome to be able to eat bananas, oranges, and even grapes. On our wedding day, in the early spring of 1954, I was fifteen and Pat was twenty-two. Being married was so different, and I was so very lonely during the day with no brother or sisters around me. I even cried a few times while waiting for Pat to come home from work.

We began having our family and had a baby every year for the first years of our married life. It was very exciting to me to see the family growing in numbers, but little did I anticipate the work or the responsibilities that were involved.

Patrick & Audrey Mabley (18 years old), with three babies & Pat's parents

Having three babies before I was eighteen was quite an experience, and then I had a fourth child before I was twenty. All this was exciting, though tiresome. Things were made extremely difficult as there was trouble with Pat, my dear husband. When Ralph, our firstborn, was about four weeks old, I had milk fever and a temperature of one hundred and five. Pat was caring for Ralph in the kitchen of our two room suite on St. George Street in Vancouver. Ralph was crying in high gear. Suddenly, there was a deadening silence. I got off my sick bed and rushed to the kitchen and saw Pat's large hand over Ralph's nose and mouth, trying to stifle the cries, I think. Ralph's little body was blue. I rushed towards Pat with all the weight of my body and pushed him away from our helpless four week old baby boy and screamed, "You have killed our son!" I then proceeded to collapse into a chair. Pat swiftly moved and picked up Ralph's lifeless little body, took him over to the sink, and turned on the cold water tap onto his forehead. Ralph's arms and legs jerked and he began to cry real loud. Ralph was alive! Hallelujah! Even then my Lord was intervening.

Almost a year later to the day, a similar catastrophe happened with our daughter, Evelyn. Evelyn was about six weeks old, and Pat was feeding her a mashed banana. I was upstairs having a bath. Again, I felt that terrible "knowing that something's wrong" feeling. I quickly got out of the tub and rushed downstairs into the kitchen, where Evelyn was gasping for air. I phoned the ambulance. They took Evelyn and me to the hospital and put an oxygen mask on my little girl. She required suction to remove the banana from her lungs. Pat had been feeding her a banana and she wasn't eating it, so he jerked her hard while she was eating to cause her to gasp, and then the banana that he wanted her to eat wouldn't go down; instead, it went down deep into her lungs.

I began to realize that there was something wrong with Pat. He was so very cruel to our babies; however, being so young, I began to wonder if I was okay in my mind. My mother's instinct told me his cruelty was not normal. Pat would tell me he was older and wiser and knew so much more than me. By the time there was a third incident with our third baby, Brett David, I decided to leave Pat. Pat did a lot of weird things. I sought help from Family Court. A Family Court worker told me that Pat needed psychiatric help.

David was about ten months old, and I left Pat babysitting. We were living in Langley, British Columbia. I had gone to visit Mom in Vancouver, a long ride of two hours. When I returned home, David was lying in his crib in a pool of dried blood. He looked like he had hit cement extremely hard. His tiny face was swollen and black and blue. Pat said he hit his face on a toy in his crib, but I knew Pat literally smashed him with his hand.

I left Pat and went to live with my mother and younger brother, Leonard, and little sister, Linda-Lou. The rest of the family had left home by now. I missed Pat, despite his problem, and when he asked me to meet him in a fancy restaurant in downtown Vancouver, I did. He was very kind and sweet and so desired for us to get together to try to make our marriage work. I agreed to get back together. Pat said he was going to Edmonton, Alberta, on a construction job, and soon as he was settled he'd send for me and the children. Pat was a caterpillar operator.

The next day I saw him off on a train from New Westminster. To this day I can still picture him waving happily, boarding the train. I never saw him alive again. Several days later an R.C.M.P. (Royal Canadian Mounted Police) officer came to my door to inform me of Pat's death. He was killed in a truck-train collision on Highway #16, near Edmonton. He was transporting the caterpillar he drove to a job site.

My reaction was one of disbelief. I argued with the officer, saying, "You must be wrong. It cannot be Patrick Maurice Kinzie, my husband." I cried like an animal. Then I looked around me and saw my little children's faces—these dear ones who had no father. Evelyn, my second child, put her small hand on my head and said gently, "Mommy, why are you crying?" I took a deep breath and stopped crying. I was determined in my heart to give them all I could, as the realization hit me that *I was all the children had*. Again, I had no way of knowing that a twenty year old widow with four little ones, aged five and under, was a tremendous responsibility.

I got a job at Hudson's Bay Company (The Bay) as "supervisor/trainee." I saved up some money, and my grandmother helped me buy a house in Burnaby, British Columbia, before I was even twenty-one. As the law stated that the house could not be in my name until I was twenty-one, the house was put in my mother's name.

After I left the Bay, I got a job at the Army & Navy department store in New Westminster. The money I received from working was twenty-two dollars per week (seventy-seven cents per hour). That plus the widow's pension of one hundred fifty dollars per month helped us to just get by. As Pat's accident had happened while he was working, I received a monthly Compensation Board cheque, which was a great blessing.

Things went along pretty well for awhile, but again trouble brewed. I had a problem getting reliable babysitters to watch over my four children. One sitter was not feeding my baby, Lily-Anne. She was throwing out the tins of baby food that I had bought, so I would think she had fed the baby. She was only troubling herself to give Lily-Anne milk—canned milk with water from the *hot* water tap. I had been so fussy with my babies, giving them fresh canned milk in sterilized bottles, with only freshly boiled water. Lily got weak. I called a doctor who told me to get some food into her or she would get scurvy. She could not even hold her head up at four months old. After this doctor's visit, the truth of what had been happening was confessed by a friend of the babysitter. She confessed to what was being done daily. This really alarmed me. I wanted to stay home with my children, but really had to work for financial reasons. The one hundred and fifty dollars per month from the Compensation Board was simply not enough for house payments, food, etc.

I joined the Army Reserve for fellowship and began drinking, having parties, and always looking for a father for my children and a husband for me. However, I was looking in the wrong places. One night I met this fellow and was telling him of my children at home. He did not believe I had four little ones at home, so I invited him over to see them. They were all asleep as we walked into the bedroom. There were bunk beds with Ralph and David sleeping sweetly, and Evelyn was in an old crib made into a cot. Then we proceeded to the next bedroom that I shared with baby Lily, who was four months old. As I was pointing into the basket, I turned around and he was gone. He had literally run out the back door and left it wide open. While this was sad, it was also quite amusing.

About this time, Bud S. came into my life. We fell in love. He was very possessive. We talked of marriage. He nicknamed me "Kitty," and he made me feel loved; I loved his possessiveness.

In the area where I lived, the buses ran only once an hour, so hitch-hiking was a common thing for me. One fellow who often gave me a lift had a friend who sold cars. I purchased one on payments. Bud, my husband to be— or so I thought—wanted to go up north, get a job, make big money, buy me a ring, and then get married. I let him use my precious car, joyfully out of love, and I never saw it again.

It was a tough world. With so many single girls looking for fellows, what chance did I have with four kids? I was so discouraged. I began drinking in the evening, and my milkman called me the "Merry Widow." I didn't mind, because it sounded happy. However, I was not getting a good reputation. My bills were piling up. My mortgage payments were getting behind, my electricity was being shut off, and I lost my home.

We moved temporarily into my grandmother's basement. My job situation improved due to the experience I had acquired at Army & Navy as a cashier. I got a job at Dominion stores (a food chain). Unfortunately, that changed as well, and I lost my good job at the Dominion stores.

My sister, Marie, and her family and I moved together into a rented house. Marie had the basement suite. I met Johnny Beckingham through my brother-in-law, George

Mooney. Johnny was quiet and lonely—a settled down type of man with a good job as a skipper on a boat. We began to live together in a big house in Surrey, British Columbia. It was nice, and I felt very wifely. Joyfully, I kept the house spotless. Meals were cooked and pastry baked. Oh, how good it felt to be in the role of wife and mother! We were planning on getting married, as there was still in my heart the sweet old-fashioned idea of marriage being special. A common-law relationship was not really for me.

I got pregnant, but my attitude towards Johnny was changing, especially when I saw him kick Ralph's little body in the back yard. There was uneasiness in me about our relationship, and when Johnny was asked to leave, he did. Ralph, my oldest, was in school, and another baby was on the way. I had apparently gone from the frying pan into the fire.

At about this time, I met a friend of a family member who knew that I was pregnant and already widowed with four babies to look after. This fellow told me about a man and his wife who strongly desired a baby, but were past the age of being able to adopt. He worked for a television station and she had red hair, like me. This touched my heart. I was blessed with so many children, and they had none. Mr. E. made very good money, and they really could provide a good home for my child. The thought to let them raise the baby I was carrying came to me at first so slightly, but as the months went by, the thought became much stronger. I thought of how little I had to offer this child, and how much more the E's could give. Gradually, the right thing to do seemed more and more evident, and it was to give this unborn child to a family who would love her or him and be able to provide so much better than I could.

I moved into a small, neat house by Scott Road in Surrey, and I quieted down totally. I went to the Catholic church, picked blackberries with my youngsters, kept a clean house, and even went to bed at night very shortly after the young ones were tucked in. However, I was so very, very lonely. Once a month, taking turns with the children, one of them and I would go into Vancouver for the day and visit my mom. The other three I left with a sitter. This was a royal treat for the children and me. How we looked forward to it. It was a mom and child "together" time.

The fellow who moved me in the summer of 1961 to Surrey, where we were now living, was quite friendly and was telling me of his older, lonely brother named Rheal Cayer. He was Catholic, spoke French, and the fellow said that I should meet him. Sometime later I did, little suspecting that again through moving I had met a "husband-to-be."

Rheal Cayer was very well built; he stood five feet ten inches tall, and he had blue eyes and dark brown hair worn in a crew cut style. He was a very lonely man. Rheal's younger brothers were all married and had children, and I felt that he wanted to catch up with them by marrying into a ready-made family.

Rheal visited me regularly all summer long. He had a deep Quebecois French accent, and it was nice having a gentleman caller. Rheal did not seem to mind that I was with child and due to have this baby in September of 1961. On a clear, sunny, summer day, as I was mixing a cake in my small kitchen, Rheal made his proposal. The children were playing outside, except for Lily-Anne, who was one year old and sitting in her high chair. Rheal said to me, "You and the kids—I'll buy that."

With Rheal's broken English, I was not sure if I had heard right, so my reply was, "What do you mean, Rheal?" My heart was pounding for joy and excitement.

Audrey, 1975 (37 years old)

Rheal answered, "You, the whole bunch," with a ges-
ture of his hands to emphasize, so typical of French men. He
said, "I'll take you all."

"Are you asking me to marry you?" I called out.

"That's what I'm talking about," was his reply, with a
sigh of relief that we finally understood each other. I was so
thrilled—ecstatic. My dream of getting married was going to
come true. I had found a father for my children and a husband for me.

The thought of checking out his character, his work record, etc., never entered my deliriously happy mind. Rheal
knew, of course, that I was pregnant, but gently he was told
of my plans to give the new baby to a couple who couldn't
have children. This pleased him, and I could see the relief
on his face. I believe this enabled me to be more serious and
determined in my thoughts to allow the couple to care for my
unborn child. Rheal pretty well clinched it when he said, "It's
up to you what you do, but as for me, raising four is plenty."

Rheal had only been in B.C. on a visit, but now he was planning to live here with his ready-made family, and he was proud to have more children than his brothers did. He was gone for almost two months. I wrote to him faithfully every day while proudly wearing the pearl engagement ring he'd given me. Rheal was going to Quebec to settle his affairs and to say farewell to his relatives and his mother. One day while he was gone, I lost my ring. How distressed I was, but after offering a $1.00 reward to the finder, dear Ralph, my oldest, then six years old, found my treasured pearl ring.

Ralph was a handsome, blond haired, blue eyed, sensible, dependable youngster, needing very little discipline. He was a joy to have. Evelyn continued to be so clean, neat, and tidy. She was Mother's younger helper, indeed. She began drying dishes at age five, standing on a chair because she couldn't reach the sink. Her neatness was exceptional; I would even find her neatly stacking the silverware in its drawer. She seemed to love to clean house with me.

David was about four and such a beautiful baby boy. He could easily be taken for a girl, as his eye lashes were long and his eyes such a beautiful blue. He was always happy, and had chubby cheeks. My sister, Marion, called him "Apple Cheeks." David seemed to come into this old world smiling and with a very happy disposition.

Lily-Anne, my baby at this time, was about two and a half. She was often found after a nap doing gymnastics in her crib with one foot on each crib side and balancing her body and hands straight up in the air. Her crib was fairly narrow, but I remember thinking that she sure had a keen sense of balance and that she would probably be an acrobat. Lily was always so kind to her Mamo as a little one. On Mothers' Day, she and Evy would bring me breakfast in bed with a flower, even if it was a dandelion.

2

TRAGEDY

I DECIDED TO MOVE TO VANCOUVER TO BE CLOSER TO MY MOTHER as I was so lonely for family fellowship. Mom lived on 22nd Avenue near Fraser Street, in Vancouver, B.C. The place I acquired for the children was an "L" shaped suite with kitchen, shower, and washroom, and a front room adjoining one bedroom that ran into another bedroom. A rather unusual set up, but it was on 26th Avenue, only four blocks away from Mom's.

The night before our scheduled move, David and I were in town visiting Mom. It was David's turn to go to town with Mom. Norm, the husband of my best friend as a teen-ager, Betty Thompson, offered to drive us home. We accepted gladly.

Tragedy struck. It was raining hard outside, and it felt so peaceful and warm and cozy in the car. I was about eight months pregnant, and David, who was now about four, was snuggled up to me and my arm was around him with my head resting on his little head. We were both asleep. Linda Lou, my younger sister, who was about fourteen years old, was in the back seat.

I awoke in the emergency department of the Royal Columbian Hospital, in shock. I was telling them that I was sixteen years old and had never been married. Then the doctor shook his head, and I heard him say that I was in shock. I immediately began to give correct information about myself, as I just couldn't bear to have them think that I was out of it. But, oh, the pain it caused to breathe! I was so sure that I was dying. It was impossible to take a good deep breath of air. Several ribs were broken. The nurses kept me out in a hall all night because of the noise I was making. I truly believed that I was dying and no one was telling me the truth. I can't really remember if an effort was made to explain that the pain was from the broken ribs that were bothering my lungs.

Apparently the accident had been caused by a woman who had been drinking and sped through a red light and collided into our car. Our car spun around and hit a cement wall so hard that the front of the vehicle, like an accordion, went into the back seat. All passengers in the front seat—little David, Norm, and myself, went out the passenger side window.

I flew under the front wheel and it spun on my chest. Norm was picking glass out of his hair, so he told me later, but he was not seriously injured. Little David was cut badly near his eye and was bleeding profusely. Norm picked him up and tried to find a house to bring him to. He was told by one woman that she did not want blood all over her house and to go elsewhere. Finally, a dear lady let David rest in her home while waiting for the ambulance. Norm, Linda Lou, and the people that were gathered around thought that I was dead. I was under the car wheel that had been spinning on my chest. Then they heard me groan. Norm said it was a sweet sound, because he knew I was still alive. He got someone to phone for the ambulance. These details were told to me much later. I found it incredible to hear from Norm that the ambulance would not take us to the hospital unless he guaranteed to pay them. Linda Lou had rolled onto the floor at the time of the

Audrey & her mother, 1993

impact and was unharmed; however, Mom and I both agreed that the shock of the accident affected Linda's school year.

I was confined to hospital for ten days, desperately fearful that I was dying and no one would tell me I was going to live. To add to these fears, a hospital doctor who came to see me gave me no assurance when I asked him whether I'd live or not. He only told me that he couldn't promise me anything. Can you imagine how my heart sank? Then, my dear sister, Marie, came to visit me. She's about one year younger than me and the one in the family that we all thought would make a good nurse. Marie checked me over from head to toe and declared that I was going to be all right. For the first time in a week, a flicker of hope entered my heart. I was going to live, and it was a miracle that the baby in my womb was unharmed. Little David stayed in hospital for a short time and was released. A dear old friend, Marilyn Embry, came to my family's aid and made the scheduled move to Vancouver for me while I was in the hospital. Marilyn also cared for my little ones while I was in bed recuperating. She also stayed on for a month to help me.

The day I arrived home was a glorious day for me. It was so wonderful to be out of the hospital and with my beloved children, but, oh, how weak I was! Opening a door even required more strength than I had at that point. If anyone has had broken ribs, you know that when you rest in one position and then go to move, the pain is very severe.

If there were any lingering thoughts about keeping my unborn child, they flew away with the condition of my wrecked body. As I was now eight months pregnant, arrangements were made for Mr. and Mrs. E. to be able to raise my unborn child and receive the baby the day I left the hospital. Grace Hospital, in Vancouver, was where my baby was scheduled to be born.

On September 15, 1961, before the full nine months were up, labour began and Jeannette Louise Kinzie was born. She had red hair and blue eyes. I loved her instantly, but was determined to carry out my previous plans. When she was around two weeks old, I signed adoption papers in New Westminster, being told that I had up to one year to change my mind if I so desired. How weary I was of fighting this world and all its problems by myself, and the bright spot in my life was the thought of Rheal coming back to Vancouver to marry me, be my Catholic husband, and a father for my little ones.

Ralph and Evy were both in school and the sweetest youngsters a mother could have. David was always cheerful—a very dear four year old—and dear Lily-Ann was now two years old. All four were blondes with blue eyes, even though they were all born with red hair like their mom. The first Sunday I was strong enough, I went to Saint Patrick's Catholic Church, and cried all through the service. Oh, how thankful I was to be alive and that my little ones were not orphans!

Rheal finally returned from back east and looked more handsome than when he had left. His crew cut had grown and his hair looked good, typically black as most French men have. I loved his accent. Even hearing a man's voice in our home was a delight. We made plans for a Catholic wedding on November 11, 1961. Even though it was Remembrance Day, we didn't mind, joking that our anniversary would always be on a holiday.

Although I was only twenty-three years old, my doctor had put me on blood pressure pills as a result of my accident. I couldn't enjoy our wedding to the fullest, because of my health, but despite it all, it was delightful. We were married at St. Patrick's Church with a beautiful service and Mass. My sister, Marie, was my witness and Matron of Honour. Rheal's brother was best man. The reception was at my grandmother's house on 19th Avenue in Vancouver. I can still remember the joy of my sisters and I preparing celery with cheese and snacks with such joy and laughter filling Grandma Sider's house (my mother's mother). We drove to Portland, U.S.A, for our three day honeymoon. Our funds were limited, but the joy that was in me at having a husband was really tremendous.

Rheal was very good to his step-children. He treated them like they were his own. He would tell stories at night, and once they were in bed, if they called for Mom, he'd go to them and tend to their needs, which usually was "I'd like a glass of water." Rheal would tell me that I had been running after them all day so I was to sit quietly. This was his way of telling me to rest. It was quite a change for me, and I hadn't realized how much the children would have me, as Rheal called it, "running all night."

As the months flew by, I began to know my husband better and began to realize just how different we were. He loved to play poker one or two times a week. Gradually, I became very interested. Having sat and watched him play for many months, I knew how to play. The first time I was asked to sit in on a hand to make up the sixth player, I won. I was hooked on poker playing. It was so exciting to me. Eventually, it got to the point that we were playing two or three nights a week, often all night. Rheal didn't work much. He insinuated that having married a widow with four children was his good deed to society, and that welfare was pretty good.

I hated being on welfare. The joy of having a husband outbalanced the disgust of being on welfare, but not for very long. I began to be irritated by his unemployment, and even made a remark that it was a wonder he didn't get sores on his backside from sitting so much.

Many things were bothering me—Rheal not working, and not having my last baby with me. I kept having this dream where I was looking for a baby that I could not find. Also, Rheal's idea of married love and romance was the opposite of mine. Even when we'd been married only a few weeks, I'd go to kiss him and he'd say, "The honeymoon is over. What is this kissing for?"

Rheal agreed to use a major portion of the car accident money to pay a lawyer to get Jeannette Louise back home with me. How my heart ached for this daughter of mine. The thought of this court case caused me great joy, for I was told that when proceedings start before the first year was up, the mother always wins.

Mr. S. was retained as my lawyer before Jeannette was a year old, but I found out later that Mr. S. himself had adopted a child and was sympathetic to the adopting parents. The case lingered on and on, and I now believe that it was so it would not go to court until Jeannette was well over a year old.

When we finally did go to court in 1963 in New Westminster (that was where I'd signed the adoption papers), it
became even more obvious to me that my lawyer was sympathetic to the adopting parents. He was quoting to the
judge, to the best of my recollection, cases where the mother
lost the child to the adopting parents. It was like being in a
nightmare. Rheal took the stand and kindly stated if we were
able to have Jeannette Louise, he would treat her like "one
his own." I was so thankful for Rheal's words, but still the
damage was done, especially since the case did not get into
court for over a year. The other lawyer found out I was pregnant with a child from Rheal, and this did not help matters
any. The judge heard the lawyer say to me under oath, "Is it
not true that in due course you will have another child?" Of
course my answer was "yes." Afterwards, I reasoned that the
only way the other lawyer would know of my condition was
if my lawyer, who'd possibly noticed that I'd put on a little
weight in my tummy, had told him, because I was only a few
months along and not really showing.

I lost the right to have my baby back. The blow, however, was eased some by the fact that I would have another
little one soon. My last child came about because my mother
had had a beautiful change of life baby girl that gave me such
a longing for a baby. I went home after visiting Mom and,
taking pictures of her bundle of joy, told Rheal that I wanted
a baby. He agreed, and it only took two months before I was
pregnant with Monique Yvonne Cayer, an adorable baby with
so much black hair that she would have needed a hair cut had
she been a boy. The nurses called her "little Frenchy."

Rheal named her Monique, and my mom picked Yvonne.
Mom said she just looked like an Yvonne. I was very posses-
sive of Rheal, I realize now, and while I was in the hospital
I didn't want him to go to his brother's place to play poker,

but he did. When I found out, I was furious. It was because he went without me, and I couldn't go because I was in the hospital. I'm being very honest, dear reader. Would you believe that when Monique was about a week old, I went with Rheal to a mixed poker game? There were three married couples, and we played until four in the morning. I even fed and burped Monique at the poker table.

Monique was not neglected, for I loved this bundle of joy dearly and would often sing songs to her and rock her for the longest time. I was also sure she was kept immaculately clean and well fed, including vitamins. Monique, my youngest, was born June 11, 1964. She was such a beautiful baby. Evelyn and Lily Ann, her sisters, adored Monique. Evy (Evelyn's nickname) was always a big sister to Lily, and now, tickled pink, Lily was to be a big sister to the newest addition to the family.

Rheal's unemployment continued to bother me. I became especially frustrated one day at the supper table, when David, who was about eight years old, said, "I'm sure glad I'm a boy, because I'll grow up to be a man, and men don't have to do anything, and women have to do lots of work." I looked at Rheal and wondered what kind of influence he was having on these children.

As I mentioned earlier, Rheal's affection level was so very, very low that I felt starved of a kind, loving word, or a hug. I can remember working so hard keeping the children's clothes spotless, ironing, and sewing. The floors in our row house (condominium style) were hardwood, and you could see your reflection in them. I spent many hours polishing them. Meals were something special with dessert every day—something I never had as a child. I even baked lots of pastry and home-made bread, but nothing seemed to fizz on Rheal, and then the inevitable happened. I say inevitable because I was so ripe for the affections of a smooth-talking man.

Rheal brought him home. He'd worked with Rheal on one of the few jobs Rheal ever had. It was a winter works program to get people off the welfare roll. It only lasted six months. The man Rheal brought home was Bill S. He began to come to our poker games and continually looked at me with adoring eyes. I was so flattered. He even followed Rheal and I when our family went to Sechelt, B.C.—a ferry ride from Vancouver—to visit my mom. He invented an excuse to always be where we were, showing up everywhere. He'd phone me constantly through the day and say things like, "With a gorgeous wife like you, I'd be afraid to go to work." He'd watch the house, and when I'd go out to bingo, he'd follow my car. It was unreal, the attention he lavished on me, and I ate it up. He'd linger after a poker game when we quit at a fairly sensible hour, like one or two in the morning— sensible in comparison to all night games. Rheal would go to bed and leave Bill and me talking in our kitchen, alone. By the time Bill first kissed me, I'd convinced myself Rheal didn't love me or care. He'd almost thrown us together, and I felt I really, really loved Bill. I now realize that it was only a physical attraction.

Rheal found out about Bill and me and laid in wait for him behind our front room door with a baseball bat. He got me to phone Bill to come over and to say that Rheal was out. I honoured his request because of the hurt in his voice and eyes, but Bill was a rounder (which means he really could fight), and Rheal was no match for him. He moved quickly and got Rheal in a position where he was literally choking Rheal to death. Something happened to me, and I saw Bill really for the first time and saw what he was really like. Quickly, I jumped on Bill and pounded him with my fist, screaming, "Leave my husband alone." He left and so did my cheap relationship with him. It was over for good. I never saw him again.

Rheal's hurt was so very deep. One day I followed him to the Ivanhoe Hotel when he had told me to stay at home. It was Thanksgiving Day, and we had company for supper. I'd baked pies and cooked a lovely meal. Ronald B., a dear friend of Rheal's, was at our house waiting for dinner. My possessiveness of Rheal caused me to go to the beer parlour to try to get him home on time for dinner. I did go uninvited, and he was still hurting. I never dreamed of the trouble I was walking into.

He grabbed me and physically threw me into his car and slammed and locked the car door. Then he got into the car, and I was headed for a ride that I'll never forget. He was driving with one hand and punching me with a closed fist with his other hand. I felt like a rag doll as I was bashed around. He must have snapped for a while. He beat me into semi-consciousness, removed me from the car, and dumped my limp body on our front lawn.

What a sight for our dear children and our guest, Ronnie, to see. Ronnie was so kind; he carried me into the house, quieted the children, and called a doctor. I had a concussion and my thoughts were so confused. I didn't even know my own phone number for days. My doctor counted twelve blows with a closed fist to my body. I didn't blame Rheal, but still we went to court and the judge ordered Rheal Cayer removed from his own house, because the judge stated that another outburst like this one—according to the doctor's report—would likely kill me. I never knew this was possible for a judge to do, but it is and he did it. Rheal was not even allowed to come to the house to pack his clothes; a policeman escorted him, by court order.

Ronnie was a dear friend in this troubled time, and I remember my sister, Marion, helping out, bless her sweetness. We'd only been married five years, and again I was alone, shattered, and feeling so very guilty. I could not say in words how guilty I felt. My body healed, but the scars in my heart were very deep. I didn't even realize it at the time, but this guilty feeling was playing havoc with me, and I felt so very worthless.

CHAPTER 3

A VIOLENT RELATIONSHIP

FRIENDS AND FAMILY ENCOURAGED ME TO GET OUT AND ENJOY myself and try to forget my troubles. The poker games pretty well stopped, and I began to go to a legion at 20th and Fraser in Vancouver. There I met a fellow in an unusual way. I thought he was a neighbour of mine, so I waved at him, and then he came over to ask me to dance. After talking to him, I realized that he was not my neighbour. He looked at me with such adoration that I felt at the time he really liked me. He was a very unusual fellow. He was extremely jealous. We went out to legions and began a romance that lasted two and half years. When I touched him, right from the beginning, I tingled throughout my whole being. Because of this, I thought I was experiencing true love. We stuck close together, and our friends would say that where you see Gerry, you'll see Audrey, too.

His name was Gerry R. He was about six feet tall, had blue eyes, and was well built with sandy coloured hair. He had a longish nose and a very kind looking face. Gerry could play guitar so beautifully—Johnny Cash style, and, oh, how I loved to sit and listen to him sing to me! Two favourite songs were "Allons Danser Collinda," a French song, and "Praise the Lord, I Saw the Light." How happy I was when he'd sing, and when he gave me a lovely engagement ring.

Problems began shortly after we met. Only a few months after we started to see each other daily, he began to smack me around. The first time he hit me, he knocked me right off my chair. It was the first of many beatings because of his jealousy. I thought the jealousy was a sign of deep, true love. Twice I went to the hospital and said I'd been in a car accident because of the beating he'd given me, and still I hung onto him as though he was my last chance at having a man in my life.

My children knew I loved them, but I know it hurt them to hear and see these problems. We were drinking quite a bit. Years later, Ralph, told me he'd often pour out our bottles of liquor half way and then fill them up with water. We never knew the difference. What a brave, sweet thing to do; he was only around twelve years old when he did this.

There were good times mixed with the terribly bad. During the good times, Gerry showered me with love, telling me how beautiful I was, and how very much he loved me and wanted to marry me, and how he was afraid to lose me. This made me feel loved, but I see now that it was a physical thing and that guilt—because of what I did to Rheal, despite the beating he gave me—caused me to tolerate the bad treatment.

In a jealous rage at the American Hotel in Vancouver, after I told him that when I was walking back from the ladies room a man made a pass at me, Gerry yelled, "Who is he?" I was scared and pointed him out. I could hardly believe my eyes. Gerry picked up the heavy armchair that he was sitting on and cracked that poor man's skull wide open. Gerry was arrested and charged with assault. Feeling sorry for him later, I bailed him out. Much later I pulled his bail, needing money for my children for food on our table, so he went to jail for a time.

Irrational behaviour was surely being shown in the name of love. At another drinking incident, Gerry picked up the chesterfield in my front room to show me how strong he was. The strength of a man who is drunk—he lost his balance and dropped the couch on my leg. I had a severe swelling of blood in my right ankle because of a broken blood vessel.

In another incident of anger, Gerry punched me right between the eyes and broke my nose in three places. About this time, Rheal and I had become friends, which really pleased my heart. Rheal and my neighbours prompted and encouraged me to finally lay assault charges against Gerry; however, he got off the assault charge. He whispered something to the judge, and then as the judge released Gerry he scolded me. He said, "Next time, lady, think twice." I realize now that Gerry must have connived with his lawyer to say he'd caught me, his fiancée, with another man. Being engaged meant a lot to me, because otherwise my conscience would not have let me have a relationship with anyone unless wedding bells were included.

Gerry did do time in Okhalla Prison for hitting that fellow in the hotel. We began to see each other again when he was out of jail, but a bit on the sly, so to speak, because I was ashamed for my children to know I would see this man after all he'd done to me.

Another incident occurred when I went to the beauty parlour to have my hair done. He was angry because I would look extra good that night at the legion. He was so angry that he came at me with a comb in his hand to mess up my hairdo. My daughter, Evelyn, stepped in between us. He grabbed her by the arm to jerk her out of his way and broke her arm. He was so shocked; his face turned white, and he almost cried, fearful I might charge him for this terrible act.

We took Evy to the hospital, and I knew now that my love for him was dying. By now, Gerry was reporting to a psychiatrist, and on his psychiatrist's suggestion, I went along to his appointments. His doctor talked to us separately and then together. While he talked to me, he told me that if I did not stop seeing this man, he would report me to the welfare agency. I was petrified. No matter how much I could think to love a man, I knew in my heart that I loved my children more and would never chose a man over my loving children. I gave Gerry his ring back and told him it was over. He knew I meant it, because he was crying. We parted at a bus stop at Main and Broadway in Vancouver. I waved a good-bye to Gerry, and our love affair ended forever.

My drinking eased up, and my children and I drew closer. Around this time I got a job as a cocktail waitress in the Terminal City Club in downtown Vancouver—hoping to meet and marry a rich millionaire so that all my troubles would be over. After being there for about four months, I found out that the members did not even date the employees—they were not allowed to. All the members of this exclusive club were very well off.

On December 1, 1971, at my little sister Jeannie's wedding, I met my next candidate for a husband. Gerry P. was a very mature man—close to my dad's age (my dad married when he was only sixteen years old, and Mom had me when Dad was only seventeen, so my dad was now about forty-eight years old). Gerry was about forty-three when we met. He had a daughter, Diane, who was very precious. I treated her like one of my own children. Gerry and Diane came to live with us on a room and board basis. My younger girls, Lily and Monique, were delighted, because Diane was just a little younger than Lily, who was now twelve years old.

Ralph was now sixteen, Evelyn was fifteen, David fourteen, and Monique, my baby, was around seven.

Gerry P. was so refreshingly strong minded and of good character. He was recovering from a heavy loss in business, and it seemed I was good for him. We had good times together. He played the guitar, and I never realized until this writing that not only did he have the same first name as Gerry, my ex-fiancé, but they both played a mean guitar.

Gerry P. would make up songs for me that filled me with joy. He'd sing about a beautiful red-head named Audrey. I believed I was in love with him and wanted so much to marry him. Since he'd already raised a family of five, with Diane his youngest still with him, I figured he'd really understand all about raising children and be ideal for me as a husband and as a step father for my family.

Even though my family was growing, I was still trying for a whole family with a father in our home. Gerry repeatedly said his first marriage ended in divorce, and he never intended to marry again. This did not discourage me; it only made me more determined to win him. He'd been living in my home over nine months, and I knew he was very attached to me, and his daughter loved my girls very much. She wished, in a wishing well at Queen Elizabeth Park, for her dad and me to be married. My girls, Lily and Monique, wished the same thing. They all told me about it. I was glad that Diane wanted me for a step mother.

There were four of us and only one gentleman—what chance did he have? I stepped out boldly after they had lived with us for a year and gave an ultimatum to Gerry: we either got married, or he'd have to move out. He still said that he wanted no part of marriage, so I tried one last thing, since he didn't appear to want me as a wife. I went to the legion without him, and he went to his daughter's home, who lived out

Audrey & Gerry Peeler. Everyone in this photo is related!

of town. Apparently, all he did was talk of me, and then his family said, "Don't you realize that you deeply love Audrey?"

He went to our home and phoned me at the legion and said, "I have an important question to ask you. Please hurry home." I didn't realize what he wanted to ask me, yet I responded and went home. Gerry sat on my couch and said, "I can't think of a future without you. I love you. Will you marry me?" I was thrilled to say yes. I'd won a real respectable gentleman, and now my home would be complete.

Our wedding day was a dreamy time. I wore a long mauve dress with long sleeves and a net over my skirt and a mauve veil to my shoulders. I thought I looked real good for my husband to be. Monique, Diane, Lily, and Evelyn were all bridesmaids, as well as Jeannie, my little sister, who I fondly call "Jean-Bean." Jean-Bean was the same age as Evelyn and Ralph, my two oldest. Gerry's grand-children were flower girls, and Ralph gave me away. He was so handsome at sixteen years old and already six feet tall!

The whole head table was related to each other. Gerry's sons, Gerry Jr. and Jim (my sister Jeannie's husband), were ushers, along with my son David. My Matron of Honour was my sister, Marie. Gerry's best man was his brother. We got married in the same Danish church my mother was married in on 19th Avenue in Vancouver.

My ex-mother-in-law, Mrs. Kinzie, came over for a visit from Saskatoon after we'd been married for awhile. She liked Gerry. Mrs. Kinzie was not always an easy woman to get to like as a person. She told me she liked Gerry, and my heart was glad. Gerry's health was bad, and I found out that he'd already had two heart attacks. His lungs were in bad shape. Once when he went to lie down for a nap after work, I found him unconscious. It really frightened me. I began to sleep with little Monique, and she loved that. Gerry didn't seem to mind. He had so much trouble getting his breath in those days that he began using a steamer. Through all of this, he never missed a day's work. He was so very reliable, and I could count on him pulling up every evening at the same time from work. This was so very different from the unstableness that was shown in Rheal.

We got along well for years, and I really settled down and enjoyed being a wife. I filled our freezer with fresh vegetables for winter and even made large batches of cabbage rolls and froze them as well. I baked and cleaned and was quite content—but trouble was brewing.

My world began to fall apart. Gerry came home from work one day, as usual, and announced that he was leaving me. I felt like I couldn't believe my ears. When I asked him why, he said, to the best of my recollection, "You are a good woman and a good mother, but I've raised one family already and your large family is too much for me. I need to be alone. I have to go." And go he did. I was so very hurt and dumbfounded. Wasn't I ever going to have a happy married life? Little did I know that this bad news of my marriage ending was only the beginning of more grief.

Within weeks, my dear grandmother, in whose house I'd married Rheal, was very sick. While she was in hospital, our family got together at the 100 Club legion. I went to be cheered up because of Gerry leaving me. My brother, Leonard, left early with his wife, Ida, who was eight months pregnant. On the way home on Rumble Street in Burnaby, they spotted a hit and run victim lying on the road. My dear brother and Ida stopped to help. While Ida leaned over to help this injured person, another car came along and hit her and ran.

She was in critical condition at Vancouver General Hospital for about eighteen hours. While we were in vigil in a special waiting room for Ida, I called home to check on the family. My son told me the news that grandmother had died. Within hours, Ida also died, and my brother's fourth child with her.

There we were—my marriage had just broken up, two loved ones were gone, and I had two funerals to go to. I was in total shock and could not even function to make meals. Family members were gathering in my home at this time of grief, and it saddens me to remember how much trouble I had functioning. My father even came in from Winnipeg with his second wife, Edith. I remember one night telling Dad my problems, and he told me to give him time to think about it and he'd try to figure out a solution and help me in the morning. Somehow, this comforted me that night, and I went to bed.

My sister, Marie, who had had the same husband, George Mooney, for about twenty-five years at the time of the funerals, was into the beer with me in my little dining room and she said, "Audrey, how come you can't keep a man?" I started to cry hysterically; it hurt so much. She apologized and I forgave her. We were a very close family and never held a grudge.

I thank God for Evelyn's boyfriend at this time, Maurice L. He brought about one hundred sandwiches from the railroad company he worked for, already prepared. I froze them, and when anyone was hungry, they thawed out one and ate it. I appreciated this because I was too disoriented to make meals. One day about a week after the funerals, my dad said, "I'll only be here about another day, Audrey. Do you think I could have some mashed potatoes?" That did it. I straightened up enough to start cooking again and gave Dad a good meal.

CHAPTER 4

CLOSE WITH
THE CHILDREN

I QUIETED DOWN AND BEGAN TO GO TO A CATHOLIC CHURCH. I was determined to be a very good woman. The bright spot in my life has always been my beloved children, and we were very, very close. Evelyn was a real organizer. Every Christmas, since she was around eleven, she'd gather money together from pop bottles and babysitting. Ralph contributed his saved money from his paper route, and they all absolutely floored me with large Christmas gifts to show their love to their mom. As well, they have always been wonderfully good children.

I recall one Christmas in particular when Evelyn was about twelve, Ralph thirteen, David ten, Lily-Ann eight, and Monique only a baby. Under the tree was such a large present for me that it was even bigger than all five children's presents put together. It was a long coffee table and had two matching step tables. Gifts like these from ones so young! They must have started saving in the summer. Tears flooded my eyes when I realized how much my family wanted to see their mother happy. One gift that tops them all was a family ring with all their birth stones on it.

It appeared that I had been given the ability to temper the sternness of my dad with the gentle love of my mom to my children, which made me a fairly good mother. We all pulled together and they never sassed me back; there was always deep family pride and respect, despite all my marital and other problems.

From the time they were twelve years old, they were taught to buy their own clothes. I did this because I couldn't afford to clothe them properly most of their lives. Ralph had a job riding his bike delivering chicken dinners for Church's Chicken. He had to wear white pants and a white shirt. He also had a paper route. Evelyn babysat and David and Lily collected pop bottles and did odd jobs for the neighbours. They were so good at making money that they were always well dressed and, to top it off, I often gave them clothes for Christmas and birthdays. Somehow I always managed to buy every one of them a new outfit for the first day of school and made sure they always had good fitting shoes. The reason for this was because growing up I usually had to wear second hand shoes that didn't fit properly and as a result my toes grew curled. They are curled to this very day.

At this time we lived at the foot of Little Mountain on Ontario Street in Vancouver in a low cost housing complex; however, my loved ones knew on the other side of the mountain there were rich people. My kids would go over the mountain and do Christmas caroling door to door and bring home LOTS of money. As I mentioned earlier, they would save their money, not only for clothes, but to buy me gifts. I was very strict about candy, and as a result they have really good teeth.

This was all very good for them as they learned responsibility and how to handle money at an early age. From the time they were little, I set the dream of graduating in their hearts, and also of making something of their lives. God blessed me with a wonderful family, and I thank Him deeply for them and for the years of good memories that I have of them all.

Audrey with the five she raised: Ralph, Evelyn, David, Lily Ann & Monique

I'm believing God to heal any of the hurtful memories that I have caused for them during my dark years when weeping endured for a night and before the joy came in the morning (Psalm 30:5b is a Bible verse God is fulfilling in my life). At this writing, Ralph, Evelyn, David, and Lily-Ann have all graduated. Ralph is manager of Traveler's Finance Company in Victoria, B.C. Evelyn is travelling around the world with Maurice with the money they saved while working. Evy works as a teacher's aide and sells Electrolux vacuum cleaners. David is a security guard, and Lily is in banking. They are all doing well. Monique is still at home with me and is sweet sixteen—a gorgeous blonde with hair almost to her knees. Everywhere she goes, eyes turn.

In June 1975, we were blessed with a new home—a co-op townhouse with four bedrooms and two bathrooms. I was on the committee that had a say in what went into these homes and got to choose the colours of linoleum and rugs. It was a dream come true. On a bright, beautiful summer day we moved into this spanking new home where no one else had lived; that was heavenly. I'm still here at this moment. God is so good. There were always enough good things happening in my life to spark and stimulate hope in me to carry on.

We were thrilled with our new home, and I was in a state of grace. This is a term that Catholics use; it means that you've gone to confession and that your sins are all forgiven and you haven't sinned since. But loneliness was ever present, and I still had a longing for love from a man—not so much as a father for my family, as they were all pretty well raised by now. Rheal, Monique's natural father, and I were good friends, and I thought about marrying him again. I even went so far as to suggest it, but he said, "I like things as they are. We'll leave it that way." I summed up that there was no hope with him.

CHAPTER 5

A NEW
HUSBAND TO BE

I EVENTUALLY MET JIM MABLEY, THE FINAL MAN IN MY LIFE. MY brother-in-law, Bud, married to my dear sister, Marion, introduced me to Jim. Jim really liked me. I was flattered, but had been through a lot of hurt, so I plainly told him that I was only interested in him as a friend, nothing more. He told me, honestly, that he would try to be more. Little did I know that this was the beginning of being in love with an alcoholic.

In my naïve heart, I still had a belief that you could only be physically attracted to someone if you loved them and were serious about them and intended to marry them. Despite all that had happened in my life, I only felt good about seeing a fellow romantically if a wedding were in the plans. I felt a fling was a monstrous thing to have, despite the frivolous way my life appeared to have been, at times. My ideas were, I thought, old fashioned. This accounts for my being engaged three times altogether, but not marrying these fellows. This alarmed me. I began to think that a fellow would get engaged to me to have their way with me. My answer to this situation was to insist on marriage plans with anyone I was seeing regularly. These ideas were in my heart despite these many entanglements. I was not as strong as I wanted to be and I realized, now, I was a very lonely, love-starved

James & Audrey, courtship days, 1975

person—not particularly physically. I was seeking in men what I realize now could only be fulfilled with a relationship with God Almighty through Jesus Christ as Lord. I was so longing for love.

For the first six months of our relationship, Jim was all sweetness. Nothing I said or did annoyed him, and he was very patient and attentive to me. He seemed to adore me very much, no matter what I did. My attitude toward Jim, at first, was very light-hearted. It didn't bother me if I got drunk in front of him or yelled at him. I caused many scenes in our first six months together. It almost seems now that it was to see if he would stay with me and care so much about me if I acted my worst. Jim drank a lot, and it was easy for me to join him, but I never could hold my liquor. I've always been the type to drink about four drinks and that's it. I'd really be feeling good, but from my fifth drink on I became loud and not always good company.

Jim was heavy into the race track scene, and I began to be very interested in Jim and the horse races. Jim and his friends had been going to the race track for around twenty years. They considered themselves very knowledgeable about the names of horses, weights, jockeys, track conditions, etc. When I picked the first and second horse on a two dollar bet and they came in first and second, I won hundreds of dollars. Jim was so proud of me and bragged about me to his friends. He told them that I had great handicapping ability. I just beamed to have handicapped (picked) horses so well.

As our relationship blossomed, the races, which had never appealed to me before, became exciting. I especially liked the buggy races at Cloverdale Raceways in B.C. Once I bet what I called my "family's number"—five children for number five and me made number six, and with Jim it made seven. No handicapping here, just luck; numbers five, six and seven came in first, second, and third—called a triactor—and this paid one thousand dollars. What a thrill for me!

By now, racing was really in my system. Jim was fair to me. If he went to the races with a hundred dollars to bet with, he'd do his best to give me one hundred dollars, also. We did everything together—drinking and gambling.

As I mentioned earlier, Jim overlooked my scenes at first. I vaguely recall being so drunk at the race track that while trying to leave with Jim, I knocked over two tables at the bar section at Exhibition Park in Vancouver. This was early in our relationship. Jim was still being kind and considerate. After being abusive to him I'd tease him, and he was still very attentive. Nothing I said or did discouraged him.

Oh, our life was exciting—or so I thought at the time. Gambling and drinking and Jim being so very loving, at first. I began to think, "Here is a man with some faults, but he really loves me, so I better wise up and treat him better." I began to be very sweet to Jim, and I believe that I really knew how to love a fellow, because I had so much love to give. I was following Jim around like a puppy at first—to the race track and bars. We even went to Reno on borrowed money from a finance company. We bought a car on payments that we couldn't really afford.

When I met Jim I owed no bills, but now they were piling up. This bothered me a lot, and I let Jim know about it fairly often. We began to fight after the first six months had passed. Our drinking and gambling was definitely getting out of hand.

Again, I wanted a wedding ring on my finger and persuaded Jim to get busy and divorce his last wife, Alice. I instigated divorce proceedings with Gerry P. to terminate our marriage. There was something very unusual in both our lives. Jim had been married three times, and we both had lost a mate through death in our first marriage. Still, we were both brave enough to consider marriage again. This would be the fourth marriage for both of us.

Our backgrounds were so different. Jim had been an only child, whereas I was the second oldest in a family of eight. I was, and still am, accustomed to sharing, whereas Jim has a tendency to think only of number one. How we came together is really beyond me. Jim had a drinking problem that began fifteen years before we met. We were both heading for serious problems.

I can remember us both going to the race track with one hundred dollars each and losing it all. I found out you could write cheques at Cloverdale Raceways, so I wrote a cheque for four hundred dollars. We were both betting and drinking at the bar. After losing this money, we both realized we were in a serious financial situation, so we cashed another cheque for one hundred dollars to try to retrieve the money we'd lost and could not afford to lose. We lost again, so Jim wrote another cheque for one hundred dollars to hopefully recover our bad losses. You guessed it—we lost that, too.

On the way home, we talked and were sobering up. One of us said, "How could we do such a thing? What is happening to us?" We couldn't understand it, nor did we know where we were headed. A short time later, perhaps weeks, we were playing a dice game called craps with two relatives of mine. We lost all we had for food except for twelve dollars in pennies rolled up in my bedroom. We'd been saving pennies, thank God. If we'd remembered about this twelve dollars while we were playing and drinking, we probably would have used that, too, trying to make, as they say, "a comeback." Gambling had reached a peak in our lives. By the grace of God, Jim landed work out of town in Campbell River, B.C. Little did I know what a mighty turning point being in this little town was to be for us.

6

NEW BEGINNING,
NEAR DISASTER

I WAS STILL FOLLOWING JIM LIKE A PUPPY. WHEREVER HE WENT, I followed. We were very close in our misery and troubles. I believe I loved him dearly, and in his way he loved me. Being away from gambling was a break for us, like a breath of fresh air, but there still was the booze. Jim always worked, no matter what he had been up to the night before. How I admired him in his strength and determination to be a good worker, and I still do admire him for it to this day.

Only Monique, my youngest, was at home now. The rest were on their own. Ralph was assistant manager at this time. David worked for Langara College, Lily-Ann at a bank, and Evelyn worked for Manpower. We made Monique come with us to Campbell River. Monique was now about thirteen years old and hated it there. This was a difficult age for Monique, but she still managed to get almost all A's in grade seven. After much grief and no success in trying to persuade Monique that she could get used to a smaller town, we finally gave in and allowed her to return to our beautiful co-op townhouse in Vancouver. Her older sisters, Evelyn and Lily, watched over Monique.

At this time in my life, I wanted to be told I was loved every time I drank—especially by Jim. He was drinking and ornery and would not oblige me. It was almost like a cat and mouse game we were playing, because I really believe now that he did love me in his way.

One night this charade was going on and I said, "Jim, if you don't tell me you love me, I'm going to take our car and ram it into a brick wall and kill myself." He said, "Go ahead. Here are the keys." He was laughing. I was furious. Grabbing the car keys, I stormed out to the car lot just outside our apartment in a two storey building in Campbell River. I got into our car; put the keys into the ignition, and then thought, "Now what am I going to do?" I'd called his bluff, and still he never came after me to tell me he loved me. In my drunken state of mind I began to think, "If he wants me to kill myself, I won't do it, because he's not worth it. He won't even say he loves me." I marched back into our apartment and threw the keys at him and huffed off to bed.

The next morning after Jim left for work, I felt terrible. I jumped back into bed, pulled the covers over my head, and thought, "I'm not getting up until I get an answer to the mess my life has become." In my soberness, I reasoned that perhaps if I'd had one more drink last night, I might have driven the car into a brick wall and done away with myself. My family, even though most of them were grown up, would have no natural mother. Oh, God ... the thought of this turned my stomach. I believe that then I called out to God to help me. The thought came to me—phone AA. They'll help me. I popped out of bed and dialed for help. A gal named Jean S. came over in less than an hour. What a sight I was, and our apartment was a mess. Jim had spilled beer on my hair and it had dried. There were empty bottles all over the place. Jean was very kind and listened while I told her my troubles. When she left, she gave me some pamphlets.

When Jim came home and I told him all of this, he laughed and said, "I've spilled more booze than you've ever drank. You don't need AA. You could be a candidate for Al-anon to learn how to cope with me, but AA? Never." I didn't want to cause problems or displease Jim at this point, so I telephoned Jean and asked her about Al-anon meetings instead of AA meetings. She gave me all the information I needed.

I was dead serious about needing help, and I quit drinking right then. I'd had enough of downhill life and was looking up, and I mean really UP! I didn't know where this would lead me.

I attended Al-anon meetings faithfully at least once a week. I remember distinctly at one meeting a sweet little Indian gal named Ruby D. She was telling us of her many woes. She had so many burdens. Oh, how sad it was! My heart went out to her. When the meeting was over and we were mingling together having coffee and fellowship, I approached her and said, "You poor woman. You have so many troubles."

She quickly said, "Oh, it's all right. I have my Lord Jesus, and I'm high on the love of God." Her eyes shone like stars. I looked at her like she was crackers, and backed off in case it was catchy. I made a bee-line for the door, and even left it open. I got into my car and drove home, but something inside my heart clicked. I thought that if Ruby could get so strong and be so happy in the midst of all her problems, it must have something to do with praying. I began to step up my praying time each morning. I was already praying for a few minutes each day.

On a trip to "the homestead" in Vancouver (which we did regularly, to see the kids), I'd picked up a Bible Grandma Kinzie had given to David in 1969. Dave was about twenty at this time. Little did I realize God's Holy Spirit was working mightily in me, drawing me to God, through the Lord Jesus Christ.

After we returned from Vancouver, I started to read the Bible. I was fascinated; actually, I was in awe. The men that I now know as the apostles seemed so real to me as I read. Matthew, Mark, Luke, and John all seemed to repeat each other so much that I thought I was reading what I had read before. It appeared to me that they were all saying the same thing as they told how it was when they walked the earth with the Lord Jesus. After the first reading, I did not realize that they were each giving account of what they saw and knew of our Lord Jesus. Of course, the accounts were parallel, for all truth is. I know this now, but I didn't know it then.

Attending Al-anon really got me thinking about God and about going to church, but where? Jim said that the only church he'd ever consider going to and trusting was the United church or the Anglican church. I checked the yellow pages and saw a lady minister's name there as co-pastor of the local United church. This intrigued me, as I thought another woman can understand a woman better than can a man. I never knew until that day there were women ministers. I telephoned her and was touched by her friendliness, but also disappointed as she was solidly booked for three or four weeks with a busy schedule and couldn't see me for awhile. She was so kind and said to me, "I can hear the hurt in your voice." I started to cry softly. She prayed for me and asked me to come to church on Sunday.

There I was, sitting on a kitchen chair by the phone in that sunny two bedroom apartment overlooking beautiful Campbell River, and wondering why I had promised to go to church. I remembered what it was like in days past—always falling asleep in church, and it had never done much for me. However, since I had promised to go, I went. Jim was very surprised. I was even surprised myself. Little did I dream of what God had prepared for me in that little church on that special Sunday.

First of all, when I walked in, Jean S., the lady from AA, came rushing over to me and with a big hug and much gusto, welcomed me. When Molly S., the lady minister I'd talked to on the telephone, began to speak, I was really in awe. She looked like a saint and radiated love, joy, and peace in her appearance and words. Her first words were, "God loves you." She said it three times. I immediately knew in my heart that God, who made heaven and earth, loved me. I felt a flip in my chest/heart area. Oh, how good even that thought made me feel! All my life I'd been looking for love, peace, and happiness in a man, a human being who has faults, and all along, God loved me. He really did. I just knew it. Right away I purposed to love back the God who loved me.

Molly continued with, "Isn't God good? We have something wonderful for you today." On and on came joyful, loving words of hope and peace, and I lapped it up like a hungry puppy. I could hardly wait to go to church each Sunday after that.

Other changes were happening. I began to really look at myself, and I wasn't too pleased with what I saw. I was determined to improve myself. I started by getting my grade twelve diploma. This strengthened my self-confidence a tremendous amount and amazed Jim. I wanted to improve myself even more and enrolled in college to complete a business office training course. I completed this venture with good marks—a B average. My confidence soared, but Jim was really hitting the bottle vigorously and was very cruel at times— not physically, but with sharp, cutting words. He called me "a Bible punching b---h."

One day I developed a skin irritation, so the doctor prescribed medication. I had a very severe reaction to this medication that caused my body to feel like it was on fire. Oh, it was horribly painful! Jim would not drive me to the hospital. He yelled, "I'm not driving you, you hypochondriac. Take a cab." Well, I did take a cab. The doctor gave me a prescription for a mixture to bathe in to stop and soothe the terrible itch.

When I arrived back home, I was weak and shaky and feeling terrible, like I was dying. Jim started in on me again, calling me names like "sissy-boob" and a lot more choice words. We didn't sleep together (one of the many nights not spent together). I was on the sofa, and I don't believe I ever felt so very, very low in my whole life. The lamp was on in the front room where I lay, and I heard what sounded like two men's voices talking in our tiny kitchenette. One said, "Let's take her now, she's ready." The other seemed to answer, "Yes, let's." Being terrified, I tried to yell for help, but could not speak. I forced myself and a gargled noise came out of me. Managing to yell "God," I heard the men's voices say, "Oh, no, she's yelling for Him. We'll get her later." I was still trying to call out for help. Noise came forth like, "Yin, Yim! Elp!" I was trying to call, "Jim, help me!"

Jim heard my noises and came rushing into our dining room and slapped me hard across the face. I was shocked, crying and hurt. Asking Jim why he had hit me, he promptly answered, "You weren't making any sense, but now you're okay. Good night." He went to bed.

I suppose he did what he could in the state of mind he was in at this time of our lives. He was drinking heavily every day, about a twenty-six ounce bottle of vodka. I've come to believe that on that particular night, my call to God Almighty was from the depth of my soul. God heard me. He began to put a song in my heart.

One day I was singing in the bathtub. Jim was planning to drive to Victoria, B.C., to go to the horse races. Later he told me that he couldn't tell me he was going to the races because I had sounded so happy. By this time, God had washed away all desire to drink excessively and all desire to smoke. It was awesome! The desires for things that were bad for me simply melted away. Praise God! What a blessing, because I know folks can struggle all their lives over these habits, especially when they are out of control, as I believe my drinking and gambling once were.

CHAPTER 7

BAPTISM OF
THE HOLY SPIRIT

JIM BEGAN ONE OF HIS MANY ATTEMPTS TO QUIT DRINKING. EACH time he tried, my heart would get so very excited, but the failures were very discouraging. So many times good food and even steak were ruined because he'd get drinking and decide not to eat, even after he'd told me to cook supper, which I did with great joy as I loved to cook in those days and loved to do things to please him. I had such a strong desire, even a longing, to get closer to God and to see Jim come to God.

One evening in the spring of 1978, Jim was getting desperate. He was almost crying and said, "I need help, Audrey. Phone AA for me." I was astonished and asked him if he really meant what he had said. He told me, "If I didn't, I wouldn't ask you." I called and two members came over. One of them was a strong man of God and very active in the United church. We'd met at a prayer breakfast that I'd been attending regularly every Wednesday morning. Unfortunately, not very much came out of their visits, which occurred only a few times. Jim was just not receptive enough at this time.

I was attending prayer breakfasts at the Haida Inn, where Jim's niece, Terry, worked. Elders from the United church were there and sometimes Jim Scott, my pastor, would be there. Dear Jean, the gal from AA who'd come to my aid many months prior, was usually there. We really had great discussions about God. I was really growing in the knowledge of the Lord. One morning I was very upset because Jim was calling me a fanatic as I was so zealous for God and desired to grow in my relationship with HIM. One of the folks there said, "Oh, Audrey, don't you know what that means? It's that you are a *fan at it*—loving Jesus." My distress turned to JOY as this was SO true now.

It was at one of these breakfasts that Bill K., an elder in our church and government agent and a very dear man of God, mentioned to me, "I believe you'd like the baptism of the Holy Spirit." I didn't know what he was talking about, but if it would make me strong or closer to God, I wanted it. The following Sunday at church, I approached Bill and asked if I could please receive the baptism of the Holy Spirit. He told me to come over to his house when I was ready. I replied, "Can I come over right now?" He told me that was fine. He didn't even mention that his dear wife, Betty, was home with a cold and in her housecoat. When I arrived, Bill and his wife very kindly prayed with me and I asked God to fill me with His Holy Spirit—a simple but powerful prayer on April 23, 1978. They were careful to have me first renounce all evil, so I could receive the fullness of God's gift of the Holy Spirit. This was according to God's Word in Matthew 3:11, John 1:33, and Luke 3:16.

Surprisingly, I never felt anything. I'd heard a friend say that she wanted nothing to do with tongues, which is a heavenly language from God Almighty that Holy Spirit filled people often receive. In my heart I wanted the fullness of the Holy Spirit to be stronger and get closer to God, but if it was all right with God, I didn't really want the tongues. I soon changed my mind.

You see, I thought nothing happened, and Betty had gently mentioned perhaps because I was drawing so close to God, He was already drawing close to me. In my heart, however, there was a big change. One night after I prayed for the Holy Spirit fullness, I sat bolt upright in my bed and shouted out, "Jesus Christ is my Lord!" I was amazed and looked around. Jim was sleeping and so was Monique, who was once again living with Jim and me in Campbell River. They didn't even wake up. The Spirit of God was so strong in me that it caused me to loudly confess Jesus is Lord.

I believe now this happened that night because, to my knowledge, I had never specifically asked Jesus Christ into my heart or confessed with my mouth "His Lordship." Now, the Holy Spirit stirred up a love for Jesus Christ in my heart that was preciously sweet and beautiful, and I wanted to acknowledge and know Him as my personal Lord and Saviour. This was both awesome and delightful.

I now believe that the basics to being rooted in God's love and family are to receive Jesus Christ into your heart by asking him in at a specific time to be your personal Lord and Saviour, to confess you have sinned and are sorry, and then to surrender to His Lordship in your life, with obedience to His Holy Word, the Bible, and move on to a deeper walk by asking God, our Lord Jesus, for the baptism or the fullness of His Holy Spirit, as it is written in Luke 11:13.

I believe when you ask Jesus Christ to come into your heart to be your personal Lord and Saviour, according to John 1:12–14, you receive Jesus and become a son of God—male or female makes no difference because the Bible refers to God's people as "mankind." I further believe that the Holy Spirit enters your heart when you receive Jesus as Lord, but not in His full capacity, because God also says in His Holy Word, Luke 11:13, that He will give to them that ask Him the Holy Spirit.

According to what is written in the Bible, we receive Jesus Christ and the fullness of God's Holy Spirit as two distinct blessings, yet with the oneness that God is Father, Son, and Holy Spirit, even as we are spirit, soul, and body (1 Thessalonians 5:23). To help me understand all this, I like to think of an apple that consists of peel, apple, and core. Three parts—one apple. Further, in Acts 8:15, 17 and 18, it clearly says that prayer was for people who were already baptized into Christ. They already knew Jesus. In order for them to receive the Holy Spirit, the laying on of hands took place and the gift was given. Acts 1:8 tells us that we shall receive power after the Holy Spirit is come upon us, and we shall be His witnesses, bearing His lifestyle in word and deed.

In closing these thoughts, it is my blessing to pray for people with the laying on of hands and they receive, what I term, the baptism of the Holy Spirit, from Jesus Christ, according to John 1:33. Jesus Christ baptizes in the Holy Spirit and with fire. Folks receive regularly in answer to prayer with the evidence of a heavenly language. I believe what Simeon says in Acts 8:18, when he says he saw the evidence of this baptism: reasoning that he saw people speaking in tongues—a new language that folks did not know or have beforehand.

Some Christian circles believe these blessings ceased when the apostles died. I respect their opinions and right to believe this way, but having gone through the whole Bible, I find no distinct words of God to substantiate this opinion. Jesus Christ said that we will do greater things because He went to the Father and sent us the Comforter, the Holy Spirit (John 14:12, 16, Acts 10:38). If the gifts of the Holy Spirit and power died with the apostles of old, how could we continue to do what Jesus did? What would we use for power?

The apostles were anointed from on high and did what Jesus did. The lame walked, the blind saw, the deaf heard, and the sick were healed in Jesus' name. The disciples were empowered from on high by the blessed Holy Spirit, and we can be also. I do today the things my Lord Jesus did. My sufficiency is of Him, and He receives all the honour and glory. The Word of God says that things will cease when that which is perfect comes (1 Corinthians 13:8), but that, I believe, is for when He that is perfect returns—the Lord Jesus Christ.

After Bill and Betty K. prayed for me, Betty told me that some people sense an awareness of God touching them, like a warm hug of love from God, and that others feel nothing in particular. However, we are still being ministered to by God Almighty. I was beginning to learn a tiny bit about the faith walk—that it does not depend on feelings. God's people shall walk by faith. Amen!

I was drawing near to God, and He was surely drawing near to me, fulfilling James 4, 7, and 8. At another prayer breakfast weeks later, Bill told me he believed that because we had asked in faith, believing God, He truly had filled me with His Holy Spirit. I believed it more and more as my walk with God deepened.

One thing I noticed within days of the prayer for baptism in the Holy Spirit was that I had a love for everyone. I was amazed when I went to a movie with Jim and Monique. As I walked into the theatre and looked at the crowd, I loved them all! I realize now that God fulfilled Romans 5:5: "*And hope maketh not ashamed; because the love of God is shed abroad in our hearts by the Holy Ghost which is given unto us.*"

Being baptized means being immersed; therefore, with the Baptism of the Holy Spirit you are immersed in the Holy

Spirit. Truly, my outlook towards people in general had changed. I felt a genuine love and concern, even for total strangers. If I saw someone crippled or obviously needing a healing, I immediately desired to pray for them.

Bill talked to me about being baptized in water by total immersion, and my heart filled with joy at the thought of it. These experiences were completely different than the Catechism of First Communion or Confirmation I had received as a young girl in the Catholic church. I had done these things as tradition, but not from my heart, so they were not truly sincere or meaningful to me.

I was still attending College to acquire my "Business Office Training Certificate." Monique was doing well in school, but Jim was not doing well. He was still drinking heavily and really was wondering what had happened to his old drinking partner. I was doing my best to be very quiet about Jim's drinking, not wanting to aggravate or antagonize him in anyway.

About this time, I met and befriended a beautiful young Christian named Brenda K. at "The Women at the Well," a ladies prayer group at the United church. Brenda also attended the United church. She was so refreshingly in love with our Lord Jesus, and when she was told of my receiving the baptism of the Holy Spirit, she promptly called Bill and Betty and went for prayer and received the same blessing. Shortly after this, we had a "Gift" seminar at "The Woman at the Well," and dear Brenda and I both received the gift of evangelizing from our Lord. We both could lead souls to Christ with awesome ease. Brenda and I were so very happy. We talked together about water baptism and were to have this joyful blessing in June 1978.

Jim, Monique, and I had gone to Vancouver for the weekend. He got very drunk and was bugging me about "being dunked in the ocean." This didn't distract from my desire to be baptized by water immersion, the same way my Lord had. Jim dropped Monique and I off on his way back to Campbell River at Willow Point. The baptism was held in the back yard of a dear Christian couple, where there was sand and the beautiful Pacific Ocean.

What a glorious day that turned out to be. Ray B., a minister from Courtney, B.C., officiated. He talked about our sins being washed away, and I felt such joy and desired to run into the fresh water to be as clean as he was talking about. I could hardly wait my turn. Five of us were being baptized, including dear Brenda. Finally, it was my turn. Everyone on the beach was singing, "And Jesus said, come to the water, stand by my side. I know you are thirsty, you won't be denied." Pastor Ray told me to hold my nose with one hand and to place the other on my chest and lay back on his arms and the arms of another attendant until I was totally immersed, laying flat as though I was lying in bed. As I lay in the water, even though it was only for a few seconds, I felt so very linked to Christ Jesus, my Lord. As I arose, it was as though a light from heaven shone on me and the brothers and sisters in Christ were now singing, "Jesus, Jesus, Jesus ... there's something about that name." Oh, how happy I was! It was like heaven on earth. Remembering it as I'm writing fills me anew with joy. To follow our Lord in water baptism is great!

Ruby D. had become a dear friend in Christ to me by now. She's the one that had all the problems at Al-anon— the one that was high on the love of her Lord Jesus. Well, Ruby was there—praise God—to share my blessed event. She came up to me and said, "The Lord quickened me to give you this as a remembrance of your baptism." She put a tiny white rock in my hand. I held it for hours and hours, and it became hot in my hand. That same evening, much later, I was in our tiny kitchenette doing a Bible study for my ladies' prayer group and the Lord quickened to me Revelation 2:17, that says. *"To him that overcometh, will I give to eat of the hidden manna, and will give him a white stone."* I was so thrilled to see described in the Word of God what I'd received.

CHAPTER 8

WEDDING BELLS

BEING BORN AGAIN BY GOD'S WORD AND SPIRIT, I COULD NOT continue to live common-law with Jim, so I told him point blank, "Jim, we either get married or split up." I really meant it, and he knew it. He agreed that we should get married—quickly. We made plans to get married. I asked Molly S. to marry us, and she said that she would be delighted. Incidentally, dear reader, we were married February 17, 1978, before I was baptized in the Holy Spirit and by water. Because we lived in Campbell River at this time, and my family was about two hundred miles away, not very many were able to come to our quickly decided wedding day.

When God touched me, He really touched me! Jim and I did not sleep together until our wedding night, and I believe that God blessed our day and evening especially because of our self-control and abstinence. On our wedding day, Jim had to drive his crane to Vancouver, about two hundred miles from Campbell River. He had to be up at four a.m. Around seven a.m., the crane quit running. Jim was very concerned, because timing was very important on this special day. Jim had to get this huge crane to town, and then fly back to Campbell River for our wedding. The crane he was driving was a forty-five ton Lorraine. He worked for Much

Last wedding—James & Audrey 1978

and Time Crane Company. Well, here he was flicking his Bic lighter because it was dark at seven in the morning. The crane was broken down completely. What to do? At this moment, unknown to Jim, I was on my knees praying. Jim fiddled with the battery connection and tried the engine, and it immediately started! He was really touched, later, when I told him at that exact time, prayers were being said for us. God was in control, for sure fulfilling Psalms 31:15.

Monique was at our wedding, of course, as were Jim's cousins, Hugh Gardiner and Sharon Motion and their families. There was a small reception held at Sharon's home, and we had a cake and a great time. Brenda was there, of course. Dear Ralph was working in Edmonton, Alberta at this time as a representative for Travelers Acceptance Finance Company, well on his way to success. I don't recall the reason why Evelyn, David, and Lily were not in attendance, but I know I wished they were there.

Audrey & Jim, February 17, 1978

The service in that lovely United church was delightful. Behind Molly S. was a large cross, illuminated with lights behind it, and this came out so lovely in our wedding pictures. How I treasure them!

Attending church on Sunday and going to my prayer breakfasts were not enough for my "hungry heart." I heard of a group of gals gathering once a week to sing praise songs

to our Lord and to pray and share, so I began to join them.
I loved it!

For ten years of my life I had had repeated bladder infec-
tions, and even surgery to tighten the muscles in my bladder
didn't appear to help much. The problem at this time was that
I was retaining water when my bladder had just been emptied,
and my doctor was very concerned. Upon a hospital visit, it
was discovered my retention level was up to the two cups, far
more than tolerable. My doctor ordered a second testing. He
said this condition was serious and another operation might
help. There was no guarantee of any success, though.

On June 21, 1978, at one of our weekly prayer and praise
gatherings, the gals and I all held hands and they prayed for
me to be healed. I felt a warmth in my lower abdomen, and
when the second testing took place in the hospital, the retention level was normal. Praise God! The Lord healed me!
My love for God and knowing how very much He loved me
was becoming so very, very strong.

I was growing in my walk with God, and then Jim's job
in Campbell River was finished. It was back to Vancouver
for Jim, dear Monique (now fourteen years old), and myself.
This was now mid-summer of 1978. I was concerned, because
just before our scheduled move back, I became very ill with
bronchitis. Monique had to do all the packing. I was so very
sick and so very sad. I cried at the thought of leaving my new
found friends in the Lord. Truly, I felt like a baby bird that
was kicked out of her nest and didn't know how to fly. My
valley was just beginning. Oh, I recovered from the bronchitis all right, but I missed the fellowship so very much.

At this time, I began to watch *100 Huntley Street*, a daily
Christian program with talking and music. They have counsellors available all across Canada to enable people to phone
in for counselling or prayer. I certainly called them often with

prayer requests for Jim's deliverance from alcoholism and gambling. Both of these problems bothered me immensely.

The revelation I received from God through the Bible, the Word of God, was awesome! I literally loved and still do love to spend plenty of time reading God's Holy Word and getting to know Him better. This was so very enjoyable to me, especially when I read that faith came by hearing the Word of God (Romans 10:17). I began reading the Bible aloud, softly to myself when others were at home and louder when I was alone. My faith soared. Prayers were being answered so fast and so often that it became difficult to keep track of them. I began to enter them in a book. Praise the Lord!

At the same "Gift" seminar where the Lord showed me that I had received the gift of evangelism, it was also discovered that the Lord had then blessed me with the gifts of faith and of intercessory prayer. With these gifts, I thought, "I can win the world." Well, the gift of evangelism was being exercised mightily. I was leading souls to Christ regularly. My daughter, Monique, prayed with me to receive Christ when she was fourteen years old in the summer of 1978, and my second daughter, Lily, prayed to receive Jesus Christ when she was nineteen years old on her birthday. Praise God! My eldest daughter, Evelyn (twenty-three years old), returned home from a trip touring Europe and prayed with me in my bedroom to be born again.

My oldest son, Ralph, came to the house when he was twenty-five and doing really well in his life as manager of Travelers Finance Company in Victoria. He came with Marcia, with whom he had been going out for about six years. In my bedroom, Marcia also quietly prayed with me to receive Jesus Christ during one of their visits in September, 1978.

Ralph came to town on a business trip for three days. I prayed to my Lord that Ralph would receive Christ Jesus as

My family: David, Lily Ann, Jim, Evelyn, Ralph,
Monique, Audrey & Jeannette 1988

Lord before he went back to Victoria. Praise God! On the
morning of the third day, we prayed together and Ralph was
born again on March 14, 1980. Hallelujah!

David, my second son, had gone to a little church in the
fall of 1978. He responded to an elder telling him about Jesus, and David prayed to receive Christ. My Lord was really
working to prove His Word that I am saved and my whole
household (Acts 16:31).

God was moving mightily on my Aunt Tilly (my dad's
sister). Oh, how the Lord touched her! Wow! We were at
"outs" for years. She couldn't stand me for a time, and I understand. She thought that I'd never amount to anything. I'd
always admired Aunt Tilly and loved her no matter what she
said or did. When I was a child, she had my admiration. She
was so very kind and helped out a lot. Actually, I believed
she was the most beautiful lady in the world. I can remember
when Carole and I were twelve and thirteen years old; Aunt
Tilly sewed us each a costume to go to a Halloween activity,

and we won first and second prize. It caused me to have a tiny inkling at that time that maybe I wasn't so totally ugly. My costume was the Queen of Hearts and had lots of white net over white satin, and I had a crown and wand with hearts all over me.

My Lord touched this lady in her fifties, and she transformed before my eyes into a mighty woman of God who loved and cared for handicapped and mentally challenged people. She still talks and prays to God throughout the day and reads the Word of God. We've been knit together in God's love so tightly.

At this writing, we are believing God for her son, my cousin, Bill W., to become "World Champion Snooker Player," and to give the glory and honour to God. For many years in a row, Bill has been in the top eight snooker players in the world. I pray for this so that people all around the world can see what happens when God is on your side and people pray, especially when a mother prays.

Next, my sister, Maria, and my mother prayed with me to receive Jesus Christ as their personal saviour. The way this happened for Maria was so precious. Mother had already asked Jesus into her heart, and I was touched to phone her long distance to pray with her to receive the baptism of the Holy Spirit. But somehow I got Maria's number by accident. Actually, it was no accident, but divine providence. Maria lives close to mother in Half Moon Bay, a delightful place on the Sunshine Coast near Sechelt, B.C. Mother has six acres of land and is with my dear step-father, Leonard Wallace, a gentleman who loves Mom very much.

I told Maria that I wanted to talk to Mother about a blessing from God and got her number instead. Maria said, "Well, whatever you were going to tell Mom, tell me." I immediately picked this up as from the Lord and we talked of the joy of being born again and receiving Jesus and of being baptized in the Holy Spirit. She responded with a strong desire to pray with me and to receive these mighty blessings and Jesus as Lord. After prayer with Maria, I was singing with joy and called Mom. The Lord through His Holy Spirit prepared her heart, and she also prayed with me to receive the blessing of the baptism of the Holy Spirit. Mama felt God's presence so strongly! She said in a breathtaking way, "Audrey, I felt like I got scrubbed all over."

Nine nephews and nieces have been led to Jesus since I was born again. Even as I write this, I am in awe. Truly, the gift of evangelism was being manifested.

I mentioned earlier how Evelyn, my eldest, received the Lord at twenty-three years of age. This is how it happened. It took place on September 5, 1978. She had just returned from a trip to Europe and was having problems with her boyfriend of five years. As she was telling me of this situation, there were other family members in the kitchen. I suggested that we go upstairs to my bedroom where we could be alone and talk. We went up, shut the door, and my heart quickened with knowing that the Lord had prepared her heart to receive the good news of salvation. After talking to her of the need we all have to desire Jesus as our Saviour and to have the Holy Spirit give us strength, she very sweetly prayed to receive Christ and be redeemed. Praise God! Even the memory of it fills me with joy. We hugged each other and tears of happiness flowed. What a thrill to see a loved one, especially a daughter, saved!

As I mentioned earlier, during the summer of this same year, David had received the Lord. While working, a terrible accident happened to him. He was struck with a two thousand pound lathe. It fell on him, and had it not been for the Lord, he surely would have been killed. But David had a praying, believing mom, and God hears and answers prayer. Hallelujah! David was struck on the eye and arm and fell over. He then got up and said to all the other employees who were shocked to see him get up, "Will someone please get me an ambulance?"

David knew that God had intervened for him. I went to the hospital to see him, and we both knew that God had spared his life. His eye was stitched and his arm put in a cast. He was told that his bone was crushed in his arm and that there wasn't too much that could be done, but with repeated operations and casts and perhaps surgical pins, David could use his arm again, but that it would never be really right again. By now, my faith was growing to the place to believe God for healing, so we gathered in my little kitchen to pray with family members and friends of David's, Brenda and Merridee. We prayed a simple but powerful prayer.

God performed the first of what was to be many miracles that have been prayed for in my kitchen. He healed David's arm while it was still in the cast. We found out about this healing when David went for his next appointment with Doctor Hock to have his arm X-rayed to check the progress. Doctor Hock was amazed and said, "Your arm had been mended." David phoned me from a phone booth after leaving the doctor's office, and breathlessly he said, "Mom, God touched me." Hallelujah! What a mighty God I serve! This victory was shared briefly on *100 Huntley Street* television in 1979 at one of their rallies here in Vancouver, B.C.

In August 1978, during an illness, my Lord Jesus quickened this thought to me, "Thou art Worthy, thou art Holy, thou art Mine." Oh, how blessed I was and as giggly as a school girl! Jesus Christ makes us worthy, having taken our sins upon His own precious body and dying for them in our place that we might be made the righteousness of God in

Christ. I Corinthians 1:30 tells us that Christ is our righteousness, and Ephesians 4:24 tells us that we put on the new man that God created in righteousness and true holiness. This rings true because God said it in His Holy Word and it is impossible for God to lie. Further, He is not a man that He should lie (Numbers 23:19, Titus 1:2, Hebrews 6:18).

I believe God's Word is literally, totally true, and this child-like acceptance by faith has brought and will continue to bring many blessings and victory to all I pray for. Our Lord said if any person be in Christ, behold he is a new creature. Old things are passed away, behold all things are made new (2 Corinthians 5:17, Galatians 6:15).

On October 3, 1978, in the evening as I was dozing, my Lord spoke to me and I wrote down what He said: "As He has power and authority over all works of darkness, so do I as He dwells in me by His Holy Spirit, and I in Him" (Psalms 68:35 and John 4:17). He will never forsake me nor leave me, for He cannot disown Himself, and I am linked to Him by His precious Holy Spirit. As I drew nearer to God, things appeared to get worse and worse with Jim, but I began to see something unusual happening. As things got rough between Jim and me, I was a drawing closer to My Lord for strength, and I began to get very, very strong.

I would receive peace that surpasses all understanding. When I'd be hurt by something my husband had said or done, by his heavy drinking and abusive words, I'd retreat to the washroom and pray for and receive strength from God. It was awesome! I could smile sweetly after even a short prayer, and even talk kindly and gently, "being loving to the unlovely." This was God's love being shed abroad in my heart—the perfect love that never fails (1 Corinthians 13:4–8), that hopes all things, endures all things, and believes all things. This thoroughly amazed Jim. He knew I was retreating and praying in the washroom, because he saw the strength I was receiving. Sometimes he'd come to the washroom door and ask, "Are you going or praying?" I was getting stronger all right, but Jim was being downright obnoxious.

It seemed that I was going through an endurance test in which Jim was being as ornery as he could be, and he was seeing if I'd stand for it, still love him, and not cave in. There were times of crying, and I remember one day when I was remembering nasty cutting words he'd yelled like, "I don't love you anymore. Anything I ever felt for you is dead." Well, at this particularly low time, the Lord quickened to me that the joke was on the enemy, the instigator of these severe problems; the more I was bothered, the more I would turn to God, and the more He would strengthen me. Even as I write these words, it is quickened to me in Isaiah 59:19, "*When the enemy shall come in like a flood, the Spirit of the Lord shall lift up a standard against him.*" Hallelujah!

A fact that I call "truth" was becoming very real to me. The more difficult the situation in my life, the more I'd turn to God, and I did not "waste my sorrow" (the title of an excellent book by Paul Billheimer), but instead praised God in every situation—not *for* the situation, but *in* it (to me there's a difference). Praising Him and thanking Him was my way of saying, "It looks bad, and Lord, even awful, but I thank You. You are in control. I'm believing and trusting You for something good to come out of this mess, and it always does." I also realized that God dwells in the praises of His people and draws near to those who draw near to Him.

The enemy hates it when we praise God, and he doesn't stick around God's praising people. Further, he's caused so much sorrow, grief, and misery in this world that it pleases me to know praises don't please our enemy. So the tougher the situation, the more we turn to God, and the more He strengthens us. The blacker the problem, the brighter the answer! The crunch of this is that the Lord showed me He is actually using satan to make His people stronger. We will not get weak through fiery trials, but stronger as we always turn to the Lord.

One day I was in a hurry to get into our car. Jim had been waiting for me, as there was quite a line up at our bank. I jumped into the car on the passenger side and hit my head on the side paneling of the car. I saw stars and received a concussion. My head really throbbed, and I had a headache all night. I learned to be more careful when I got into a car, but the Lord spoke to me through this incident and said, "We learn through pain, at times." This is not by His choice, but it's how we are as human beings. Few people look to God until they're in trouble, but I believe that as we progress in our walk with God, He can and does teach us many things by the total leading of the gentle Holy Spirit and the Word of God.

It takes awhile for us to hear and know God's voice and to be totally open to Him. The more I listen to my Lord Jesus, the keener my ear is to hear Him. Holding grudges and being unforgiving mainly harms us by blocking some of the blessing of God to us, and also the grace to hear God's Voice, do His Will, and be led by His Holy Spirit. Even in the Lord's Prayer that Jesus Himself gave to us to say, clearly it says, "*forgive us our debts as we forgive our debtors*" (Matthew 6:12).

9

STRENGTH AND WALK BY FAITH

THERE IS STRENGTH COMING DOWN FROM GOD TO HIS PEOPLE, those who know Jesus as Lord, which is truly awesome. This strength allows us to have peace no matter what is happening around us. Christians are to walk by faith, not by sight, and not being moved by adverse circumstances, for when we trust our Lord and love Him, as I do so very dearly, it is true. According to Romans 8:28, *"All things work together for good to them that love God and are called ..."* I believe all believers are called. God never said all things were good, but He said they'd work to good. Perhaps some of them will work for our eternal good, because He also said that if you suffer in well doing, your reward will be great.

My daughter, Evelyn, had tears in her eyes when I told her not to worry about Jim treating me so badly. I told her, "When Jesus calls me forward to receive my rewards, Evy, you'll be there to see it. So will Jim." I believe God for this victory. I began to realize these truths were real, and I could feel the strength from daring to believe God said what He meant, and meant what He said! I also had a great peace in knowing who I am in Christ. I came from God, I am going to God, I belong to God, and I know this is real. I'm only here as a pilgrim, and my real home is in Heaven where my heart is with God, and where I'll live in joyous happiness forever and ever with my Lord Jesus.

The real truth is that when we have peace in our hearts from God, then our peace and strength will not be based on a happy marriage, a good husband or wife, a good job, money in the bank, etc., but on our relationship to God Almighty. This is a key to a walk of faith. The man or woman who will say, as I have, that they will not be controlled or greatly moved by situations or problems but by the Word of God and what it says, will have mighty strength from God— to the extent to cause people around you to be amazed. This was a secret of Paul's strength! He said, *"But none of these things move me ..."*

God loves us each and every one of us, and what He's done for me, He wants to and will do for anyone, because He loves us all equally. I have been at peace when my husband yelled at me, "I no longer love you. I'm leaving you and you'll get no support from me." When there is no money in the bank and I'm down to my last five dollars, the Lord has touched a total stranger's heart to mail me over one hundred dollars (bless her dear heart). I've had folks come to me and say, "The Lord told me to give you this," and place money or a cheque in my hands. I know God loves me and He is supplying all my needs according to His riches in glory through Christ Jesus my Lord. Trusting God is continually becoming a way of life for me.

On October 22, 1978, my Lord enlightened me that He heals and answers prayers in Jesus' name in His time, as we wait in "faith," hold fast to our confession of faith, say to people, "I'm believing for thus and thus," and look to our prayers to be answered. This pleases God, because faith pleases God.

In faith believing, I thank God for Jim's deliverance from alcoholism, gambling, smoking, and all evil. Even if he's in a pub drinking, or drinking at home, or at the race track, I'm still believing for victory in his life. I'm not lying, but exercising faith. Non-Christians generally say, "I'll believe it when I see it." Christians believe it, and then they see it.

10

TRULY, I DO THANK GOD THAT I MARRIED AN ALCOHOLIC

ON NOVEMBER 23, 1978, I CAME TO REALIZE THAT I COULD SAY, "Thank God I married an alcoholic." It has turned me to God. In my misery, I began to seek God and found a delightful faith walk with Jesus Christ as Lord. I've learned through this difficult situation to lean on and walk with God, totally depending on His strength and promises to me in His Holy Word.

I'm learning patience in all areas of life, and compassion, love, and peace beyond normal human understanding or strength. Through it all, I've received the grace to trust and depend on God completely. I no longer look to Jim for my peace and security, but I look to God, who is so very much more dependable than a human being.

I began to hate the sin Jim was involved in, but to love him, the sinner. The man I love would be bothered by the enemy tempting him to do all the things he hates which cause guilt and hostility to be directed at him, and which are taken out on loved ones such as me. When he's attacked by all this hurt, he surely doesn't need me to bug him or add to his misery. No way. Through Jesus Christ, my Lord who strengthens me, I will generate love to him (1 Corinthians 13:8). I firmly believe evil cannot persist indefinitely where God's unfailing love exists. There is the odd exception, granted, but we pray, believing for victory in all situations, and leave the results to God. God is love and He has conquered evil on the cross of Calvary. Jesus Christ, my Lord and Saviour, got us the victory!

I began to realize something even more precious. If I held bitterness or anger or resentment towards Jim, no matter how much he may have deserved it, I was only hurting myself. It wouldn't hurt him, but would block the channel of God's blessing and strength to me. I needed all God's strength for the difficult task ahead. So I would say to my Lord, "I will forgive him and anyone who has hurt me in *your* strength," because some people inflict hurt so deeply that you cannot forgive in your own strength.

On November 30, 1978, Jim left home again. In answer to prayer, along with my dear daughter Monique, who was growing strong in the Lord, I received the peace that surpasses all understanding. We stood in awe, because we were not upset. I still loved Jim and had compassion for his suffering, but I knew I was under God's umbrella of protection. It was as if there was a wall of love surrounding me and protecting me from falling apart.

I continued to live day by day, always managing to have funds for food and living expenses, knowing God was providing for us sometimes in miraculous ways. I'd like to describe some of them to you. A brother in Christ named John came to my door and told me, "My mother said the Lord told her to give you this." It was a twenty dollar bill, and at that point we were down to our last few dollars! Another miracle occurred when a retired man insisted that we go to the bank and open a joint account into which he placed thousands of dollars. He instructed me to take out what I needed for monthly living expenses. This carried me over for many months. When that ended, I reasoned with the Lord

(Isaiah 1:18, 19) that I needed at least two thousand dollars per month to live respectfully and raise my daughter. Miraculously every month it came—sometimes a thousand dollars, six hundred, five hundred, and sometimes in smaller amounts of fifty or a hundred dollars, mainly from people who knew me and went to my church.

Then my church began to give me a salary of six hundred dollars per month, for a year or so, and then raised it to one thousand dollars. The rest came in elsewhere. I believe this was because He called me to work in the ministry. He would supply my needs. This provision was strong confirmation for the call in my life.

I was also a tithing woman of God. I gave ten percent to God's work, and this obedience caused my faith to soar. The ninety percent went further and I walked under open heavens. I still tithe to this day, and the ministry does as well. Amen.

At a time prior to these miracles, my daughter and I were once low on groceries and I had an overdraft on my back account. I went shopping for food using the overdraft. When I got home, I received a phone call from the very store I had just shopped at, telling me I had won a contest, and the prize was a $150 gift certificate! I was amazed, realizing that if I'd just waited a bit longer, I wouldn't have had to use the overdraft. I shared what had just happened with my daughter, telling her I hadn't entered a contest.

"Mom," she said. "I know that because I entered your name."

There began to be a pattern to Jim's comings and goings. I'd go after him when three or four weeks had passed and coax him to come back home. I'd tell him how much I loved him and that we'd work things out. Then he'd come home and try to be good for a few weeks, sometimes even a few months, but eventually he'd fall back on the booze trail and leave again.

On December 3, 1978, Jim called to ask me to come see him in the motel where he was staying. This motel has since burned to the ground. Jim's voice was desperate, and he told me he thought he was dying. He asked me to please come to him, which I did. He was deathly sick and very afraid. He told me that if he got any sicker, he would commit suicide. I stayed all night with him and quietly prayed most of that night. He was sweating and very hot, throwing up violently. He had the runs at the same time. It was a terrible sight to see.

He poured out half a bottle of rum.

"Alcohol is poison," he declared. "That ruddy stuff tried to kill me. To hell with this garbage! I'm joining AA or something."

The next day, December 4, 1978, Jim came home sick, sober, and sorry. Our prayers had been answered! All day I rejoiced. Jim stayed home quite a spell this time, and he made a New Year's resolution to control his temper. Things were going along fairly smoothly, and I was still drawing closer to God, realizing that the troubles I have in life—the problems with Jim—were actually responsible for my having a deeper relationship with my living God, God Almighty. This was such a wonderful reality. Even when things were going well, I still desired to pray, read the Bible, and have fellowship with God and His people. In trying times you develop a love relationship with Holy Father through the Lord Jesus, which deepens when the good times come. Praise God!

Rough times were no longer a problem, because I trusted in God to work it out and to strengthen me while I waited for victory. During difficult times of Jim's unreasonable behaviour, I continued the habit of retreating to the washroom to pray. Jim knew I was praying, because when I came out there was an aura of peace around me. You see, dear reader, he was never told that I was praying, but he figured it out.

God was showing me many wonderful things. For example, the Bible became very personal to me, and every time I read a powerful verse, which I now call "promises," I would ask God in Jesus' name for the promise to be for me personally. In 2 Timothy 1:7, Paul says that God has not given a spirit of fear, but of power, love, and a sound mind. As I'd read this verse, I'd say, "Father, in Jesus' name, I claim this promise for me. God has not given me the spirit of fear, but of power, love, and a sound mind." I believed these promises were for me as a born again Christian once I had claimed them: *"Whereby are given to us exceeding great and precious promises: that by these we might be partakers of the divine nature, having escaped the corruption that is in the world..."* (2 Peter 1:4).

The bigger blessings and strength came when I memorized scripture, and when I felt cast down I'd quote God's words aloud. When people were around, I'd think of the verse that I'd memorized. Soon I had enough verses memorized to suit any tough situation I found myself in. Praise God!

One of my favourite verses was, *"Greater is He that is in you, than he that is in the world"* (1 John 4:4b). I also liked *"All things work together for good to them that love God and are called according to His purpose"* (Romans 8:28). I'd always put my name in the Bible where the Lord's words said "ye" or "you" in the old King James Version. I first started reading the Living Bible and then graduated to the King James Version. I personally find the King James easier to memorize, but we are all individuals and unique, and so much loved of our heavenly Father.

Family members continued to be "born again," asking Jesus into their hearts to be their Lord and Saviour. My brother-in-law, for one, was proud to be an atheist. One day in December, 1978, he was visiting and I was sharing about Jesus.

"I want to ask Jesus Christ into my heart, but please don't tell anyone," he said.

I believed that now he would allow me to, as he is deceased. Jesus entered his heart as Saviour that day.

His daughter, my dear niece Laurie, prayed with me on the telephone to receive Jesus Christ. Laurie's little brothers, Kelly and Bradley, came to my home for a day's visit while their mother, my dear younger sister, Marion, moved into a new home. We had a great day, listened to Christian records, and talked of God and how Jesus died in our place, bearing our sins so we'd be made whole. Bradley and Kelly both very sincerely and sweetly asked Jesus into their little hearts.

Prayers were being answered almost on a daily basis. For example, Ralph sold his car for a very good price. David also sold his car, and lost things were being found. Jeannie, my little sister, got an apartment at the price she could afford and in the location she wanted, near her best friend. Monique and her best friend, Chantale B., prayed with me for Mr. B. (her father) to quit drinking, and he quit. Hallelujah!

Dear Monique's attitude towards fellows was changing. She was drawing close to God, and the Holy Spirit was doing a mighty work in her. It was so wonderful having two Christians in one house, because the Bible says in Matthew 18:19 that "... *if two of you shall agree on earth as touching any thing that they shall ask, it shall be done for them of my Father which is in heaven.*" This promise is powerful and encourages God's people to agree together. All God's people need to agree together. All God's promises are very powerful, especially when you step out and believe them.

With the life I'd had, it is no wonder that I was a chronic worrier. I worried about everything and anything. It was a bad habit, and it would drain my energy and get me down both physically and mentally. Even when I was little and

Mom and Dad would go out, I'd often stay awake until I heard their car turning into the driveway. This sound assured me that they were home safe. As my folks would enter the house, Dad would call out, "It's okay, worry wart Audrey. We're home safe and sound." My precious Lord Jesus knew all about this, of course, and one day several years after I'd been saved, He gave me a revelation or parable that turned me away from worrying. I've resolved through Christ, who strengthens me, I will not worry anymore.

What the Lord quickened to me was this—after you've prayed about a situation and you've given it or a person to the Lord, to worry about it denotes a lack of trust, and can literally remove some of the faith-believing power that's at work for the prayer to be answered. An amusing parable He gave me showed a similarity to not being allowed to fish in a pond. You might see a "No Fishing" sign. Well, when I'd begin to worry, it was like there was a "No Worrying Allowed" attitude in my mind. Praise God for victory over worry! Trusting God was continually becoming a delightful way to live. He is faithful to help in every situation.

My Aunt Tilly, my father's sister, was born again and filled with God's Holy Spirit. She and I were close after years of her hard feelings towards me. We'd pray together often and really praise God for prayers answered. She changed from a woman of fifty-six years old, filled with problems and complaints, into a vivacious, strong, mighty woman of God. She talks to our Lord daily and praises God often. He's answered our prayers in many awesome ways. For example, she was full of arthritis. Her legs had large holes in her bones, but after prayer she could work and get around marvelously. God has blessed her with faith. Once she had a severe financial problem. After prayer, she "took a notion" to take a bracelet that she thought was costume jewelry into Grassie's

Jewelers to see if it had any value at all. They valued it at four thousand dollars. She excitedly phoned me to praise God. There wasn't even a gold stamp on that bracelet.

About six months later, there was another financial need. Her landlord had given her notice, without just cause, to vacate. After prayer, her son, William W., North American snooker champion who is still in competition for the World Champion each year, came home from England for a visit. At the airport, he gave dear Aunt Tilly three thousand dollars and told her he'd back her financially to buy a house so that she would never have landlord problems again.

This woman really amazed me, but I knew it was God's strength in her that enabled her to work night shift at New Dawn, a home for mentally handicapped young people. At her age, and bearing in mind that she weighed around two hundred pounds, this was really something. The greatest blessing of all is that she really loved those patients like a mother and with the love of God. She cared for these troubled ones with such deep love from her heart, and they knew it and loved her dearly. God continued to give her strength to be kind and gentle no matter what situation they were in, whether it was epileptic seizures, bringing up all over themselves, or dirtying their beds. These beloved people were cared for by this dear woman of God with a tenderness that only God could instill in a person, and I give Him all the glory.

11

WEATHERING ANOTHER STORM

JIM HAD STARTED DRINKING AND GOING TO THE RACETRACK again. He was becoming extremely irritable, and at times he didn't make sense. What was alright today often was not alright the very next day. I knew there was a fight going on within him. He'd try to quit drinking, but when he'd lose the battle, the guilt and remorse that he felt was terrible. By this time, my ability to pray wherever I was, and also reading God's Word, had built me up to be very strong in God's strength. I was completely able to love the unlovely; I was able to love Jim no matter how he was acting. This floored him and was actually difficult for him to handle, let alone understand. He'd yell and scream, rant and rave, and I'd speak gently, softly, and lovingly. It really unravelled him. He saw such a contrast in our natures. I'm sure it made him very conscious of something out of place within him. Once it came back to me that he had told a friend at the racetrack, "Audrey is something else. She never gets mad at me, no matter what. She is like an innocent child."

One day, Jim came to me and said, "Audrey, I'm leaving you. You're a good woman; you haven't done anything, but I need to find myself. It doesn't make sense, but I can't live here anymore. Don't ask me to explain this. I just can't live here." He packed his things and left again. God once more blessed Monique and me with the peace that passes all understanding.

My Lord quickened to me the verse, "All things work to good for those who love God." I knew it was God's perfect plan for Jim to be away for the present time. God began to do a mighty work using my home. He'd lead people here for baptism of the Holy Spirit, or for prayer for needs. Praise God, He was blessing me with leading souls to Christ!

Oh, how happy I was with only God to answer to for my deeds and no longer an irrational husband! There was no way I'd allow myself to feel guilty about this joyous existence, because I knew and believed with all my heart that Jesus Christ was also with Jim, doing a mighty work in his heart and life, and in my allowing him to come to the place to really turn to God.

God, in His Mercy, was sparing Monique and I from the sadness of seeing Jim go downhill fast with his partying, drinking, and heavy gambling. I thank God that, to my knowledge, Jim never had any relations with another woman, despite his faults.

At home in this lovely four bedroom, full basement, two bathroom co-op, Monique and I continued under the umbrella of God's love and protection. We changed one of the bedrooms into an office for me, mainly to write this book for you to read. Jim was very delighted when I told him of my desire to write a book of my life story. He even approved of the title and bought me a typewriter and a desk.

Monique and I continued to grow in grace. We were close to God, able to communicate well, and both had a strong love for our Lord Jesus. He is to Monique what she needed from a father. Jim and her natural father, Rheal, were not meeting her needs in this area. He was meeting my needs, as well, for love. I was strongly learning love, acceptance, and forgiveness. Loving no matter what, accepting people where they were at, forgiving always, and forgiving everyone.

My Lord quickened to me Isaiah 54. The whole chapter ministered to me and spoke to my heart. Even at the beginning, Isaiah talks of a barren woman, and I can no longer have children due to an operation. "*More are the children* [spiritual children that I've led to Christ] *than the children of the married wife, saith the Lord*" (Isaiah 54:1). In verse two he says, "*Enlarge the place of thy tent* [open my home to the needy around me]." Verse three says, "*Thou shalt break forth on the right and left and my seed shall inherit the Gentiles* [enlargement of the ministry]." Verse four says, "*Fear not, for thou shalt not be ashamed; neither be confounded, for thou shalt not be put to shame: for thou shalt forget the shame of thy youth, and shalt not remember the reproach of thy widowhood anymore.*" I was very ashamed of my youth, and I'd been a widow. Verse five continues, "*For thy maker is thine husband; the Lord of hosts is His name; and thy redeemer the Holy one of Israel.*" This meant a lot to me, and it lifted up my heart to think Jesus Christ would be to me a Holy husband and meet my need for love. He's more than enough, my blessed Redeemer! I have grown to realize that no man can meet a woman's full need for love. Nor can a woman meet a man's need for love, because they are imperfect.

Verse six declares, "*For the Lord hath called thee as a woman forsaken and grieved in spirit, and a wife of youth, when thou wast refused, saith thy God.*" I was originally a very youthful wife, as you know, married at fifteen years of age. Verse seven says, "*For a small moment, have I forsaken thee; but with great mercies will I gather thee.*" I realized the trying of my faith was more precious than gold. God was teaching me to live by faith, not feelings, and teaching me to believe on Him, even if I didn't feel His presence for a time, so that I would learn the faith walk. Verse ten says, *"For the mountains shall depart ... but my kindness shall not depart ..."* Problems shall leave me, but God will always be with me granting me peace and kindness. On and on the promises touched my heart. Verse seventeen says, *"No weapon that is formed against thee shall prosper."* Amen!

On February 1979, I was at a check-out at the Super-Value food market in Champlain Mall in Vancouver. I noticed the cashier was favouring her left arm. I asked her what was wrong, and she told me it was very sore and hurt to move. With love, compassion, and boldness, I touched her arm.

"I'll pray for you to be healed," I said.

She looked at me kindly and thanked me so very much. Her name was Jean. Days later, I went through her check-out again.

"My arm is just fine. Thank you for praying," she said. My Lord had healed her. Praise God!

Through talking with my sister, Marion, I discovered she had received Jesus Christ at the age of twelve, having prayed with a Salvation Army worker. Now I understood why Marion had more strength to be moral than I'd had. She had God's strength. I told Marion that I wish she'd shared having received Jesus with me. However, I've learned not to despise my youth, because now it can all be used in a testimony of the strength and power you receive to change your life for the better after you are born again, and especially after you are filled with God's Holy Spirit. I sure don't keep quiet about my Lord. In fact, one of my greatest joys is talking about Him. He has brought me up from the pit into a beautiful place and into marvelous strength and peace. I know that the God who made heaven and earth is on my side and nothing at all can separate me from the love of God which is in Christ Jesus my Lord (Romans 8:37–39).

The day after Jim left in February 1979, on a sunny Saturday afternoon, I went to Marion's home to pray a prayer of agreement. I especially wanted to pray for the Lord to continue to mightily draw Jim to God. Just before we started to pray, I noticed Marion's hurt, swollen finger on her right hand. Knowing she was bowling in an important tournament (we were on the same team) that very afternoon, I prayed for her bowling and for her finger. She wanted to win and receive a day at Harrison Hot Springs, a resort up country. My dear sister really needed a day out. I knew it, and so did our Lord. We held hands and prayed for each other. Well, she not only bowled, but she won! She won "Champion Queen of the Lanes Tournament." We were thrilled for her and for our team, because we won the team championship. Later in the week, Marion was having X-rays taken for her back. She asked the technician to check and see if it was all right with her doctor, because she wanted her finger X-rayed, too. They did X-ray her finger and found that it was broken. Our Lord had left the evidence of the break for Marion to know more fully the power of prayer and how very much God loves us and even cares about little things. Marion bowled tremendously with a broken finger, and that showed the power of God. I want you to know that she continued to have no pain at all, even as the finger healed. Amazing!

I don't understand the great difference in people's reactions to God's working and answering prayers. I am always thrilled to hear of prayers answered and healings, but I am aware that it makes some people nervous. One person even told me that it scared them. God is answering our prayers because He said He would. Jesus said, "*Whatsoever ye shall ask the Father in my name, He will give it you*" (John 16:23). I have the deepest holy reverence for the Holy name of Jesus my Lord, and feel a cringe of sadness whenever it's used in vain.

When Jim left this time, he informed me that he didn't love me anymore. I had always treasured the thought of how much he did love me. Jim was always telling people of his love for me. He had told my daughter, Evelyn, twenty-five years old at this time, and also my brother-in-law, Marion's former husband, of how much he loved me, but he sure wasn't telling me. Truthfully, I was sad and there were tears flowing on and off for a few days. I was truly feeling crushed because I thought he loved me no matter how he acted, and that meant something dear to me. I'm not feeling hurt at this writing, for the Lord has healed me of that hurt, but I know it happened because I've made notes since early 1978, and my notes tell of my despairing valley. I also know Jesus my Lord was with me in this trial, but I didn't always feel His presence. It was a heavy trial, but praise God, my Lord says in 1 Peter 1:7 that the trying of my faith is more precious than gold.

God's grace is sufficient for me, and He will lift me up because I humble myself and pray often (1 Peter 5:6). My Lord placed in my heart a burning desire to speak for Him, and I even dreamt about it. I earnestly prayed for God to open doors for me to speak and tell of His marvelous love and strength. He began to open doors, and I'm waiting for more to open for me. God is teaching me to walk deeper into a total faith walk, and not by sight or feelings.

CHAPTER **12**

LEARNING THE
WALK OF FAITH

THROUGHOUT THE SUMMER OF 1979, THE LORD PATIENTLY AND lovingly led me into a deeper faith walk. I continually thought with my mind and said with my mouth that I would not be controlled by feelings, emotions, or by my old nature (who I was before I became a Christian). I also spoke out that, by faith, my old nature, called "the flesh" in the Bible, is crucified with Christ Jesus my Lord. I believe I am a new creature in Christ Jesus my Lord. Old things are passed away, and all things have become new (2 Corinthians 5:17, Galatians 2:20).

God was continuing to renew my mind daily, and I began to think God's way. God was beginning to speak to me throughout the day with Bible verses. At first I thought it was me practicing the memory of scripture, but the Lord quickened to me that His written Word mixed with faith was becoming the living Word of God in my heart.

On February 24, 1979, I persuaded Jim once again to return home. There was some evidence of God's working in his heart. Little things that he'd say meant so much. He'd use the name of Jesus our Lord in vain and immediately say, "I'm sorry, Lord." Once he said, "If God wills it, I'll quit gambling, like you have, Audrey." I continued to believe God to work a miracle in Jim.

Around this time I heard a terrible noise late one night. It sounded like a car hit our home. I jumped out of bed quickly called on my Lord, and for Jim to come and check downstairs with me. A car had rammed into our home just under our kitchen window, with some of the metal jammed into our gas meter. Jim opened the back door and saw several young fellows putting beer bottles into our garbage.

"I'm going to call the police," I called out.

Immediately, they all ran away. Thank God no one was seriously injured. Later, one came back to face the police. What a commotion! An emergency hydro unit had to come out due to the danger of the gas leaking. In about four hours things had settled down. I sure knew I had the love and forgiveness of God in my heart, because the thought that came to me was they sure needed to know my Lord Jesus. Praying for them was a joy. The insurance company paid for the repairs to our home, but I believe those three young fellows will be in heaven with me. The Lord allowed them to hit this particular house, because He knew I'd pray for their salvation.

On August 26, 1979, the day before my birthday, the Lord gave me a blessed revelation and I'll write it to you exactly as I take it from my notes of that particular day. This day the Holy Spirit led me into praying deeply for an inner healing. I asked God, who is the Alpha and Omega (the beginning and the end), to go back to when I was first conceived in my mother's womb and free me from the original sin and all evil from then to this very day. I loosed the blood of Jesus Christ to cleanse me and purify me of all sin. I took authority and cast off, in Jesus Christ's name, all the works of satan, and I put on Christ. I loosed Jesus Christ's holy healing power upon my whole life.

I asked for the Holy Sprit's filling and power upon me from the very beginning of my existence, and I brought all my members into the obedience of the Word of God, in Jesus' name, for by his stripes I am healed. It is done—a finished work by faith believing. I am totally delivered in Christ, for Christ is now all and in me (Colossians 3). The Lord was working in my life. I confessed that I will stand through Christ who strengthens me, and stand on the Word of God for my healing and deliverance, all my days. Praise God! Amen!

When I was through praying, I felt so good, so uplifted, and was moved to pray the same prayer for dear Jim, and later for other members in my family. I encourage you, dear reader, to pray this prayer and be greatly blessed.

I believe that Jesus Christ is the Alpha and Omega (Revelation 1:8), the beginning and the end. He can go back in our minds, our memories, our conscience, and our sub-conscience and heal and mend every hurt and broken place that would bother us today or in past days. God can do anything, and all things shall be possible with Him (Ecclesiastics 3:15a, Hebrews 13:8).

The marvelous outcome of this prayer was that about a month later, on September 22, Monique and I attended a "healing seminar" at Camp Kakawa, in Chilliwack, B.C., sponsored by the Cliff Avenue United Church in Burnaby. The guest speaker was Joan James of Vancouver. She was teaching on what the Holy Spirit had said to me in my heart. What a confirmation!

I realized that God was speaking to me in a very special way. One time I was driving with Jim, heading north towards the mountains on a foggy day. It came to my mind, "See over there, where the mountains are—you can't see them, but you know they are there." Such it is with prayer. Then it cleared a bit and again the thought, "You see part of the mountains now. With prayer, at times you see only a little at first. Continue to wait on God and you will see all of it. Believe it before you see it, and you will see it. Faith pleases God."

On April 5, 1979, Monique and I went to see our family doctor, W.A. Rivers. We thought there wasn't anything wrong with either of us. Monique probably just had a cold, and I thought perhaps there was something amiss in one of my breasts. What our doctor told us would have really upset us if we didn't know our Lord Jesus. Monique was told she had a serious affliction, similar to bronchial pneumonia, and he said there were two lumps on my left breast. He was very concerned and said that they must be removed by a surgeon. I was very peaceful and calm, praise God, and so was Monique.

I prayed with my two daughters, Evelyn and Lily, after they felt the lumps so that they would know what lumps felt like. A counselor from *100 Huntley Street* also prayed for our healings. Monique's chest was totally cleared. God healed us both! On April 19, 1979, when a surgeon examined me, I had no lumps in my breast. On this very same day, in answer to prayer, Aunt Tilly's son won the first round with John S. in the competition to be world champion snooker player. What a joy it was to have God answer prayer! So faith building! God continually was blessing me by allowing me to lead souls to Christ, to pray a simple but powerful prayer to ask Jesus Christ to come into their hearts and be their personal Lord and saviour. People were steadily being born again of the Spirit of God.

This is a prayer to receive Christ as Lord into your life:

Father, I believe that Jesus Christ died for my sins and God raised Him from the dead. I confess my sin and I'm sorry. I ask Jesus Christ into my heart and life to be my personal Lord and Saviour. Jesus Christ is my Lord. Amen. (Please say this prayer out loud)

What a joy to introduce folks to my Lord Jesus, who has lifted me up and turned my life around from turmoil into a marvelous joyful walk of love in Christ. I'd find myself singing the days through with this wonderful new strength flowing through me. Jim's heart was softened to be really nice to my Christian friends who would visit me from Campbell River, especially dear Ruby D. and Brenda K. While Brenda was over for a visit, we were gaily chatting about God and Christianity. Jim had been drinking, but was not drunk. He came into our little kitchen nook, and glanced over at Brenda and I sitting in our dining room on our colonial kitchen chairs.

"How can I receive Jesus as my Lord?" Jim said loudly.

I looked at him and, believe it or not, I actually chuckled and told him we would talk about it when he was not drinking. This annoyed him

"I haven't drunk hardly anything, and I can talk about this if I want to. Now, tell me what words I should say," he answered.

He was very firm and strong in wanting to receive Jesus.

"You acknowledge that you believe Jesus died on the cross for your sins," I humbly said.

"I believe Jesus died on the cross for my sins," Jim said loudly.

Then I told him to acknowledge that God raised Him from the dead, and Jim repeated that.

"I've sinned, and I'm very sorry, Lord," he said.

Then I told him to simply ask Jesus Christ to come into his heart to be his Lord and saviour. He did and was born again of the Spirit of God according to John 1:12. Jim received Jesus, and God gave him power to be a son of God, born of God. Jim also confessed with his mouth the Lord Jesus and believes that God raised Him from the dead (Romans 10:9). He is saved! Hallelujah! How hopeful and happy I was.

A humbling thought came to me: "I am becoming very strong in the Lord, because I'd been so very weak on my own strength." God's grace is truly sufficient for all of us, because His power is made perfect in weakness (1 Corinthians 12:9). We need never think, "It's impossible for me to be strong. I'm too weak." God takes us in our weakness, and He makes us strong, as He did me, by pouring His strength and life in us. Hallelujah! This new confidence that I had in my heart enabled me to take the position of supervisor during a government election here in Vancouver, and it wasn't even difficult.

My mother is a sweet little lady, barely five feet tall, and very gentle. She came from Gibsons, B.C. to Vancouver (she had to take a ferry) to see a specialist about an ear problem. We were all concerned it was something very serious. Thank God it was fairly minor. I can still remember parking my car at Little Mountain Park on a beautiful day as we prayed together. God's peace really filled Mother. My Lord blessed me with leading my own mother to Christ, to know Him as personal Lord and Saviour, and to receive the baptism of the Holy Spirit. My mother's sweet comment after praying for the baptism of the Holy Spirit (in answer to prayer) was, "Oh, Audrey, I feel as though I've been scrubbed all over, so very, very clean." Mama was sixty-four years old.

On May 8, 1979, on the spur of the moment, Jim, Monique, and I decided to go visit my mother and Len, my step-father. The trip was seventy miles and included a ferry trip. Mother and Len lived on five acres of land, and it was so very peaceful, just like a park. As we left Vancouver, I never dreamed what God had prepared for me at Mom's. I walked in the front room where my little sister, Jo-Anne, was sitting with several books opened in front of her. One of the books looked like a Bible. Jo-Anne looked very heavily burdened. I asked her if she thought what she was studying was right. She was studying Mormon philosophy. She answered me with a very concerned look on her face.

"I don't think so, Audrey," she said.

I asked her to go with me to her attic bedroom so we could talk. She quickly closed her books and followed me upstairs. We went hand in hand, like two school girls going somewhere special. We talked together and I told her, with joy, about God's love for her. I continued sharing God's plan of salvation—how Jesus died in our place to pay the price for our sins. I told her how we can be washed clean in His precious blood. I told her how God is holy and cannot look at sin, and that Jesus Christ as Lord and Saviour links us to a holy God (Habakkuk 1:13).

Jo-Anne understood we have all sinned and come short of God's Glory (Romans 3:23), so Father sent Jesus (God in the flesh) to die in our place for our sins, and if she received Christ, and asked for forgiveness of sins, she would be forgiven and receive eternal life, Amen. Then God could bless her and welcome her into His family. Joey's eyes were wide with joy, and she prayed and asked Jesus Christ into her heart.

"Oh, Audrey," she said after the prayer, "I feel like a big weight was lifted from my head." We hugged each other with a new-found closeness, one in Christ's love. The weight of guilt left her—and can also leave you, dear reader.

In June, 1979, in order to keep me humble so I wouldn't look at people as though I was better than them, God brought to my mind that I should hate the sin with perfect hatred, but I should love the sinner. My Lord Jesus came not to condemn, but to save and I could do no less (John 3:16–17). My strong desire was to shower people with God's love. Through the Lord's strength, I was determined to give the perfect love that never fails (1 Corinthians 13:8), the love that is not boastful, proud, or jealous, that rejoices not in sin but rejoices in truth, that bears all things, endures all things, hopes all things, and thinks no evil. There was an outpouring of this love into Jim, in God's strength, of course. For a long time I made the error of forgetting to not rejoice in sin, as whether Jim was going to the racetrack or out on a drunk, I'd smile sweetly and wish him a good day. Jim began to think there was one set of rules for me and another for him, and he acted like he could do no wrong.

After many months of this, it dawned on me that I needed to say, "I don't like what you're doing, but I still love you." Jim needed to know that I knew right from wrong and stood for what is right. I also knew the Holy Spirit was working on Jim, and still is doing a might work in his heart, mind, soul, and life. This is my confession of faith and what I believe to see with the eyes of faith, despite incidents to indicate otherwise.

13

MIRACLES

IN AUGUST, 1979, THREE BLESSED THINGS HAPPENED. GOD really opened my eyes to see His power and His love. On one occasion, Monique and I drove into a garage to get gas for my car, a beautiful 1973 blue and white Torino Brougham that was totally paid for. I pulled up in front of an unleaded pump, saw my error, and put our car into reverse to back up to the regular gas pumps. I did not notice that Monique had opened her door on the passenger side. As we backed up, the door was rammed by the unleaded gas pump and bent out of shape. The door would not even close. I called out to my Lord Jesus.

"Monique, shut the door," I said.

"But Mom," she replied, "it's broken." She tried anyway and it closed. The Lord had instantaneously fixed our car door. He cares so much, and he knew that it upset me to think about telling Jim about the incident.

The second miracle happened on August 4, 1979. I was awakened from a sound sleep and thought of Ghislaine V., my friend of eighteen years. I began praying for her and her family. The next day on the phone she told me she and her family had been at a wedding and she had gotten into a terrible disagreement. When I told her of my being awakened to pray for her, she was really touched to know that God loved her so much to even awaken someone to pray for her needs.

The third miracle occurred when a friend of mine, Ingrid, was very sick. Katy W., a powerful sister in Christ, and I prayed for Ingrid to be healed. The Lord healed her and gave her a vision of Katy and me praying for her. Jesus told her that Katy and Audrey's prayer was the reason He healed her. I was so very delighted to see how much our Lord wanted us to know the power of prayer.

On June 20, 1980, Jim and I were asleep in bed. At about 5:30 a.m., I was awakened with a calling by a powerful, majestic voice saying, "You are called into the most Holy priesthood." My heart pounded. I slipped out of bed, put on my slippers, and went downstairs to our dining room, so very excited, and asked my Lord to confirm this calling in the Bible—and He did! He quickened to me many scriptures, including Psalms 22:30. I knew I was going to speak for God. About a year earlier, a very special thing happened that has impacted my life ever since.

On June 9, 1979, the Lord quickened in my heart, "As I called Aaron to speak, so have I called you. Speak to my people. Tell them: 'Prepare ye the way; prepare ye the way for the coming of the Lord.' I am coming soon. I will greet my people in the air. Cleanse thyself and be ready.' Thou will speak to My people and be anointed by Me. They will listen. Prepare ye the way for the coming of the Lord. Light your lamps. Be flaming ministers for me. Jesus is coming. Our Lord is coming. You will speak to my people, child. I will prepare the way." I was so delighted to hear these precious words. Many prayers had gone up to my Lord Jesus in regard to my speaking for Him.

Jim had been gone for some time now, and I was growing in strength increasingly. I was filled with loving kindness and walking with God—not before Him, nor behind Him. I was showing His love in a peaceful way.

On July 12, 1979, I was reading God's Word while sick in bed. It comforted me. I realized that He was lovingly teaching me many things: knowing that I am in His care, fearfully and wonderfully made by God (Psalms 139:14), created in His likeness and for His pleasure (Revelation 4:11), and realizing we must all be beautiful to God, because He made us how we are.

Around this time, there was a strong tendency on my part to preach to people, especially family members, because I was so very concerned that folks would grow in Christ. It was becoming clear to me, however, that my purpose is to love first, to comfort, encourage, be kind, gentle, teachable, patient, wise, quick to listen, slow to speak, but bold to speak as I ought to speak (James 1:19). This was easy to write down, but it has and still is taking me much time to learn this lesson well. Even at this writing, there is a longing to always approach people with love, especially family members.

By August, Jim had again returned home. We decided to go away for a weekend to try to recapture the closeness we once shared. It was a good weekend. The weather was just delightful. There was a blue sky and it was very warm. We drove to Penticton, B.C. and stayed two nights in a motel, ate out, and were at peace with each other.

There were signs of God working in Jim's heart. Whenever he used Jesus' name in vain he continued to tell the Lord he was sorry. Early one morning, I said "Jim, you know I've quit gambling, so I won't be encouraging you to gamble." NOTE: I said this once before!

"If it's God's will, I'll quit too," he answered.

These small incidents were music to my ears. I was so very hopeful, believing God for a miracle. However, many troubles were ahead of us. Jim did not have victory over alcoholism or gambling by a long way.

My heart was continually encouraged by my Lord and dear Christian friends, especially Doreen H., a *Huntley Street* counsellor, and dear Anne S., a close sister in Christ. She came to my home regularly on Tuesdays for prayer and share meetings. Being thankful for the little signs of God's work helped me to see that God was working in the hearts of those we were praying for. This was so, even if we did not see evidence of it. God knows and works in the hearts of the people we are praying for.

One more precious incident occurred after a very grumpy morning farewell. Jim called me from work to apologize. I just about fell over! Some people can say "I'm sorry" very easily, but Jim never could. In the years we've been together, I can only remember about two times when Jim said "I'm sorry." God truly was working in Jim's heart and in mine.

14

THE PEACE OF GOD WHICH
SURPASSES ALL UNDERSTANDING
(PHILIPPIANS 4:7)

IN SEPTEMBER, 1979, JIM LEFT HOME AGAIN. ONE MIGHT THINK with so many comings and goings that I would have become immune or accustomed to this way of life; however, anyone who is married to an alcoholic knows that this roller coaster type of life can be very devastating. Being married one day and having a husband to submit to and answer to and then not having a husband at home the next day is very difficult to adjust to. Sometimes I'd feel like a bird let out of a cage that needed to learn how to fly again—and fly solo, at that.

Had I not known the Lord, I feel sure there would have been a serious toll on my nervous system. However, regardless of the state you're in when you receive Jesus as Lord, He can restore you to perfect soundness, spirit, soul and body, as He promised in Joel 2:25. He can restore the years that have been messed up in our minds and life. Christ is our healer (1Peter 2:24). God was healing before Jesus even came. In Jeremiah 30:17, Father God promises to heal our wounds and restore our health. Lord Jesus came to bind up our broken hearts and heal us that are bruised by life (Luke 4:18).

Even though Jim was gone, Monique and I were once again blessed with God's marvelous peace that surpasses all understanding. I remembered, again, that all things work together for good for us who love God and are called. I believe all born again believers are called and that God has a plan for our lives. One thing for sure—I knew I loved God with all my heart.

On the same day Jim left, to uplift me, God blessed me with leading an old friend of about twenty years to receive Jesus Christ as saviour. Aunt Tilly continued to be a blessing to me. We talked together often, and God was constantly answering prayers for us. We often rejoiced together. The bright spot in my life these days, was the joy I received growing in grace and seeing God work in lives, especially seeing dear people being born again. A soul winner's joy was truly a great honour and blessing.

In October, 1979, I once again went to Jim and persuaded him to return home. He did come back home, and he was trying to be so nice. He sure was sickly, as he always was every time he left home and returned. While Jim was gone, I enrolled in Bible College and was learning about God's holy Word. It was wonderful to study the Bible; however, after Jim came home, it became increasingly difficult for me to arrange time for studying. Finally, I quit college. My heart was quite sad, because I'd started something and didn't finish it. I believe now that God had other plans for me. Before I left college, a sister in Christ was led by our Lord to pay twenty dollars towards the purchase of a Bible I'd ordered. This really touched my heart.

Around this time, I began having blessed dreams. In one dream, I was being told, "My power is in My people," and I was praying and laying hands on someone. Another dream was of Saint Paul in a prison, but the prison was more like a tremendously ugly dungeon. There were chains on Paul's hands and feet, but he was filled with the joy of the Lord. He was singing and praising God, seemingly oblivious of his surroundings and situation. Paul wrote many books of the Bible from a terrible prison. He wrote powerful words of God as he was led by the Holy Ghost. Paul was strengthened mightily by our living God. He knew that God said in His Word that the works Jesus does, we will do also, and there is no partiality with God, meaning He loves us *all* the same (John 14:12, Romans 2:11). The strength and power he gave Paul, and that our Lord Jesus had, God wants to and will give to His people. In Colossians 1:29, Paul says he laboured (worked) according to God working in Him. Amen! I firmly believe this truth with all my heart; however, there appears to be a purifying, trying time beforehand for God to be sure of our steadfast faithfulness to Him. It doesn't happen overnight. We grow from faith to faith (Romans 1:17), glory to glory, strength to strength (2 Corinthians 3:18, Psalm 84:7), as we follow Christ sincerely.

Another dream came on October 29, 1979. I was walking among freshly picked fruit on a beautiful green hillside. There were bananas, peaches, apples, grapes, and pears ... all manner of fruit in clusters. I was in a cabin with two very kindly men. One was talking to me, and as he did, my knees felt like butter. I was so very shy, and shifted like a school girl from foot to foot. He asked me why I drank coffee. I told him that I really didn't know, but that it was probably just a habit. I looked outside the cabin window and saw a porch with no railing and a still, peaceful lake surrounding our cabin. I was thinking of how beautiful it would be to dip my feet in that cool, clear water. It was my custom that, upon awakening from a dream, I would ask my Lord what the dream could mean to me. The first one has already been explained—we can have strength like Paul had. The second dream meant to me that through the ministry of Christ in my life, there will be much fruit—many good things breaking forth on my right and left hand. In the last dream, perhaps God was saying that coffee is not really good for me. It has no nutritional value, and most of us know this. As for the peaceful, still water? "*He maketh me to lie down in green pastures: He leadeth me beside the still waters*" (Psalm 23:2).

One sunny afternoon, I walked into a Royal Bank on Kingsway. It was June 15, 1979, and there in the line-up was a fellow that was the leader of a band that I knew in the days of my former drinking with the legion crowd. I'd often seen this fellow on Saturday afternoons at the Kingsway and Joyce Road Legion in Vancouver. He was very popular in those days, but here and now, he was a man obviously troubled.

We talked and I knew he needed my Saviour. He shared that recently he had given up drinking. I shared the love of my Lord, and we prayed right there in the bank. He was born again of the Holy Spirit of God! He got more than he was banking for—Johnny Z. received the gift of eternal life. Praise God! He was really moving in my life.

Jim promised to go to church with Monique and me, and he did. How thrilling to us! It felt like a dream had come true. Truly, all things are possible with God. Jim had always stated that he would never set foot in Kingsway Foursquare Church, but he did. God was moving in our lives, and I loved it.

About this time, my relationship with Doreen H. began to deepen considerably. She is such a very gently thorough person, wise in the wisdom of God. She is a very precious lady of our Lord Jesus, married with a very stable, happy marriage. She and Les have raised two youngsters, Mike and Stephanie, in the ways of the Lord. Through prayer and gentle counsel from Doreen, it became clear to me that in some areas of my life—with Jim, in particular—I was being overly gentle in my love. God has a balance in everything. At times, in my desire to do things just perfectly, I would go to extremes. With

Jim, I simply poured love unto him, which is not bad, but my dear husband was in error about his drinking and gambling. I would say nothing but simply smile sweetly. This was not good for him or me. As I mentioned, Jim was thinking there was one set of rules for him and another for me. I could do nothing wrong, and everything he did was all right, even if it was wrong.

God began to show me through dear Doreen that I needed to exercise a stronger, firmer love in Christ's strength. I began to say things like, "I don't like what you are doing, nor do I think it's right, but I still love you." Doreen called it "tough love." Jesus came not to condemn, but to save (John 3:17). We, his people, should do nothing less. We need to think and, at times, say that we don't approve of sin, but we still love the sinner. Everyone needs love, acceptance, and forgiveness.

I began to realize that I was receiving guilt that was not mine to take. It was revealed to me by the Lord and through Doreen that most of my life I had taken punishment unjustly with a low self image. I was like a kicking post, believing that true love wouldn't mind people walking all over or even trampling me down. Well, I mind, but I will still forgive and love! I determined at this time to walk in God's strong love— His tough love.

CHAPTER 15

OFF TO A MOTEL

ONCE AGAIN, JIM LEFT HOME TO GO TO A MOTEL. THE MERRY-GO-round was still turning. I felt God wanted me to go to Jim and tell him I looked upon him, now, as a friend only, and he could not expect from me wifely privileges in love making. When I arrived at his motel, Jim was watching television. As my words flowed out, he turned and looked at me with obvious hurt and anger. I told him how it made me feel even cheap to chase after him in a motel, and that my relationship was now as a friend only.

I was tempted to retract my words when the expression on his face was so explosive; however, I held firm.

"I'm going to the Legion to look for a honey," Jim retorted.

He leaped off the bed and stomped into the washroom to shave and get spruced up to go out. This time Jim would be away from home the longest time of all—about one and a half years. I went home and had a peaceful night's sleep, because I was obedient to God's leading in tough love.

A powerful pattern was developing in Jim's coming and going as it pleased him. I was quite determined to quit chasing him and coaxing him to return home. After seeking counsel, it was conveyed to me in such a strong way the amount of hurt Jim was suffering, and tears started to roll down my cheeks. I began to realize that Jim was hurting as well as me.

We prayed together again and he said so strongly, "I mean business. I want to try God's way, and tomorrow I'm going to join AA."

I gently, but strongly, reminded Jim that he was born again because he asked Jesus into his heart, and that the enemy, satan, was trying to pull him down. I reminded Jim that greater was Jesus in him than the enemy in the world (1 John 4:4).

After three months of staying away from liquor and attending some AA meetings, Jim fell off the wagon and began drinking very heavily again. He was so terribly irritable and abusive, continually calling me a "Bible punching b...h," because I loved to read the Bible.

Another terrible incident occurred when Jim demanded that my dear daughter, Evelyn, not be allowed to come into our home. He had a disagreement with her about the use of a tire that belonged to him. He couldn't seem to forgive and forget, and he acted like he hated her. Once again, I was taking some lesson to extremes—the lesson to Christian women to submit to their husbands (Ephesians 5:22). Now, the Lord knew it didn't appear right to me to say this to my own daughter. But, in obedience to God's Word, I did it and believed God to swiftly touch Jim's heart to change his attitude toward Evelyn. I did not count on dear Evelyn being as hurt as she was. She did not understand what I was doing. I don't blame her for being very, very hurt.

I told Evelyn on the telephone, which made it even worse.

"Evelyn, for a time you're not allowed to come over," I said. I was going to explain why, but Evy burst into tears and sounded like her heart had broken. Even at this writing, there is deep emotion in my heart at the memory of this. Instantly, I felt as though my heart had broken to have my daughter hurting so much. I love my family so very much, and at many times in my life, especially before I knew my Lord Jesus, they were all I had, as all my other relationships were always breaking up.

Evelyn's nickname is "Princess," because she was that to me. She helped me tremendously when the family was small, and I'd fondly call her "my right arm lady." She always had our home spic and span whenever she babysat, and anywhere else she babysat. She was so neat and tidy that at school the teacher asked her to go from desk to desk to show the other students how to arrange their desks. At seven years old, she was already doing all the household chores. Evelyn was, and still is, a great blessing to me. God is healing us both of this bad memory. In fact by faith, He already has.

I hadn't counted on Evy not understanding what I was doing. Diligently following God's word to the letter was being drawn to an extreme here, and I had not learned how to balance God's holy Word. I truly believed that God would protect us, as he did with Sarah in the days of old when Abraham lied and said she was his sister instead of his wife to grant him favour—but putting Sarah in danger. God protected Sarah from all harm.

Later that day, God touched Jim's heart. He came home from work and said as soon as he walked in the door, "It's not natural, the request I made about Evelyn. She is welcome here anytime." God made the breakthrough, and to this day Jim has a new attitude towards Evelyn. I asked Evelyn's forgiveness and thank God that our relationship is still very precious and close. Even though my balance was way off, God still honoured the attitude of my heart. He is so very wonderful, and His grace covers our weaknesses. Truly all things work to good. He knows my heart and knows that I did not purposely set out to do harm.

I'd like to share how the Lord gave me balance about submitting to my husband. The words "as it is fit in the Lord" came to my mind, then a little louder down in my spirit, and then it was like a light turned on and I realized that, Yes, I submit, but only "as it is fit in the Lord." I marched into the front room to tell Jim my new discovery. He was astonished. "Doesn't it say somewhere in that book you are always reading, 'submit to your husband'"? he said.

"As it is fit in the Lord," I answered. I told him that from now on I would only submit to him if I was sure it pleased God. I was liberated in that area of biblical balance.

Sometime in December 1979, after several months on the wagon, Jim began to drink again, gamble, and be miserable and downright ornery.

"I'm leaving you, Audrey," he declared. "And there will be no support for you or Monique." I was forty-one years old at this time in my life, and I'd never really worked steady for any length of time; therefore, there was no real work record for me to use as a reference.

Relying totally on my Lord was my only recourse. I talked to Him, and at times through tears, I'd say, "You promised me, Lord, that you'd look after me. I will believe in Your Word to supply all my needs" (Philippians 4:19).

Later the same month, Jim came home from the racetrack and was sitting on the edge of our bed.

"I really don't want to go, Audrey," he said. "I'll stay and try to make a go of our marriage." We talked in a deep way that was very, very rare for us and very peaceful. I wrote in the notes that I keep, "I will believe God to restore our relationship totally and have His way in our marriage. I'm continuing to believe God for Jim's total deliverance."

CHAPTER 16

PAIN AND HEALING

ONE MONDAY MORNING, VERY EARLY, I AWAKENED WITH PAIN IN my abdomen area. There had been pain there for several months, off and on, but this pain was so bad that I was unable to move at all or even lift my head. I called Jim to get an ambulance and off to the hospital we went. Due to my Lord's strength, I was not afraid. The pain persisted off and on until Wednesday night. It was so fierce in my stomach that the night nurse gave me two pills the strength of 292's plus Valium and still the pain was terribly intense. At 12:30 a.m., she telephoned my doctor and he told her to give me morphine. The morphine did not kill the pain.

By this time the nurse appeared quite annoyed. She acted as though she didn't believe me. The pain was so intense; it felt worse than the labour of all my children. It was as though there was a war going on in my tummy. There was no use calling the nurse anymore, so I rubbed my hand gently over my tummy and praised my Lord softly into the night. With tears gently falling, I believed my Lord to act, and was wise not to question His ways.

Around 5:00 a.m., the pain abruptly stopped and I was healed. Praise God! I got up and had a shower and sang praises to my Lord. I was so groggy from all the medication I'd had that I did not cancel the impending exploratory operation scheduled for the following morning. The operation proceeded on schedule, but of course they found no abnormality. My Lord had healed me. This was one of many healings He's done.

Jim's efforts to make a go of our marriage were short lived. On January 22, 1980, Jim said, "I don't love you and I'm leaving you." I admit this was crushing news for me so soon out of the hospital. Even though God had healed me, there was weakness from the anesthetic and exploratory operation. My Lord quickened to me that I was in a valley, but in this furnace of problems, He was with me, whether I felt His presence or not. The trying of my faith was more precious than gold. God's grace is sufficient for me (2 Corinthians 12:9, 10). He was strengthening me through my problems.

I had a burning desire to speak for my Lord that was within me and being suppressed. I began to know in my heart that speaking for my Lord would come to pass. God would open doors for me to speak and grant me this desire, because I believe He put it there. I longed for God to use me in a big way as His earthen vessel to win people to Him. Oh, how I love my Lord and the love is growing every day! My love for Him grows sweeter and sweeter as the days go by.

At this time, Monique's natural father, Rheal, came back to Vancouver to live. He had been living in the States. We met him for a snack at MacDonald's, and I shared with him the love of Jesus. Being raised a Catholic, Rheal believed all he needed to believe to ask Jesus into his heart, but he so needed to take that step so that he'd be born again of the Spirit of God Rheal willingly prayed with us and received Jesus Christ into his life. Monique and I were exuberant with joy. Another family member joins the family of God!

I fully realize now that since prayer was said for me to be baptized in the Holy Ghost according to Acts 1:8, 8:15–17, there has been an increase in strength and power from God in my life. I knew the Holy Spirit entered into my life when I was born again, but this was a baptism, an immersion in the Holy Spirit that was a mighty important step in my walking as a victorious Christian, sailing through my problems, totally in Christ's strength (John 1:33, Matthew 3:11).

Another realization came mightily to me. I needed to surrender all my life to Christ, my Lord, for if I hold anything back, then I won't have the full blessing He desires for me. I've now discovered that if Jesus Christ is not our Lord, then the enemy (satan) will trouble us more. What a sobering thought! No wonder I am pleased for Jesus to be my Lord and long to see others receive Christ as well. I don't believe anyone on this planet really desires satan to rule them and take them to Hell with him, especially when we can have eternal life through Jesus Christ as Lord (Romans 6:23). There is no other name under heaven by which we can be saved (Acts 4:12). There is only one way to a heavenly existence on this earth for eternity and that is through Jesus Christ as personal Lord and Saviour (John 14:6).

I know now that being a Christian does not mean I will no longer have problems. My entire life needs to be done in my Lord's strength. Nothing can separate me from my Lord (Romans 8:38 and 39). He will never leave me or forsake me. What good news for a sick, dying world. I, who am saved, born again of the Spirit of God, am only here as a pilgrim on a short journey. My real home is in heaven where my heart is (Hebrews 11:13).

17

FREEDOM
FROM GUILT

WHEN YOU HAVE A PARTNER OR RELATIVE THAT HAS A DRINKING problem, it's easy to put blame onto yourself for the situation; to feel guilty is one of the main reasons for depression and mental problems. Leading psychiatrists all agree that guilt is one of the biggest reasons for problems with our minds. I have heard it said that if there was a cure for guilt, over half the mental hospitals would be emptied. I believe this is true.

Since receiving Jesus as Lord and Saviour, I have been set free from guilt. The way I have come to acquire the victory is to think very deeply and allow this truth to penetrate my heart and mind: "Jesus died for my sins and guilt that I would be made the righteousness of God in Him." The sin situation and guilt is settled once and for all as I follow my Lord and the leading of the Holy Spirit. I will not feel guilty.

To allow any feelings of guilt to remain while I am following my Lord is to partially deny the full work that Jesus Christ my Saviour did on the cross for me and for all who will truly come to Jesus. In Jesus' name and strength, I determined never to feel or allow guilt to trouble me, through Christ Jesus which strengthens me.

Jim was at home now, and I continued to draw close to God. Whenever things got rough, I would continually retreat to the washroom, or sometimes the bedroom. I continued to "thank God I'm married to an alcoholic," believing God to totally deliver Jim, as He had me.

Jim was becoming increasingly irritable after several months on "the wagon," and that New Year's Eve was a very unusual evening, indeed. Monique and I had gone to a church service. I promised Jim that I would leave before midnight and be home with him to bring in the New Year together. It was a sacrifice to honour my words and leave the service, as it was a very anointed, blessed service. Upon arriving home, I found Jim was in bed already, but not asleep. After a few very sarcastic remarks, he told me to leave him alone. It would have been easy to be very annoyed, after leaving the church and the celebration that was to follow after midnight to come home to a husband who would not even talk to me. But being strong in my Lord's love, I went to pray to Him and brought in 1980 on my knees.

It was a precious time with my Lord. His presence was so very dear and strong. In my notes of this special time, I wrote: "January 1, 1980: Beloved Saviour, I brought the New Year in praying to You. I have been richly blessed, and Father, this year I pray that in 1980 I will be your love vessel to all I come in contact with; family, or otherwise. That all will see Christ in me and hunger and thirst to know you as Saviour and Lord. Holy Abba, my heart's desire is to speak for You; You have given me a love and boldness to witness, and I believe a tongue of the learned. Thou give me words to say of comfort and love. I believe You will open doors for me to fulfill the desire of my heart to speak. According to Your perfect will, You will lead me by the Holy Spirit, and I am yielded totally to Your leading. I have denied myself and walk in the Spirit. The law of life in the Spirit of Christ Jesus has freed me from the law of sin and death (Romans 8:1, 2). Hallelujah!

I use this freedom for Your Glory, Lord." Little did I realize what great things God had in store for me in 1980.

God continued to root me even deeper into my rock, the Lord Jesus Christ. Another trial soon came along, but in the midst of tribulation, peace surrounded me along with an ability to rejoice from my heart as Saint Paul did. This was awesome! It was amazing I wasn't shook up about it.

The latest trial started when Jim told me he was leaving me again. My future looked so unsettled, but by faith it was going to be all right. I knew my Lord was going to perfect things which concerned me. On February 5, 1980, Jim left, telling me, "You're a good woman and it's nothing you've done. Maybe I'm going crazy, but I have to go." It was almost like he was being driven. He was a pathetic sight.

We parted as friends, but little did I know this departure would last ten months. All other times he was away no more than two or three months at a time. What transpired in this next ten months was awesome. First of all, I made up my mind through Christ who strengthens me that I would not go after Jim again. If he came back, it would be because he wanted to. I believed that this way he would be more sincere in his efforts to do what is right, and that thought made me want to stick by my resolution.

During the whole ten months, we never did without anything. God was true to His Word and supplied all our needs in every area. In the financial area, we prayed that we would never need to be on welfare, and Jim agreed to send three hundred per month. It was not enough to live on, but it was a beginning. Money came in such unusual ways. Someone, perhaps an angel, deposited three hundred dollars in my bank account. Money came in via the mail. God led people who did not even know me to assist me. I know they will receive a blessing for being obedient to my

Lord's leading. Our Lord said, *"Give, and it shall be given unto you, good measure, pressed down, and shaken together, and running over..."* (Luke 6:38).

The fact that God was using me was the most awesome blessing of all. People were receiving Christ as Lord and Saviour. Hallelujah! Prayers were being answered almost daily and being written in a book—my prayer answer book. Folks were being healed in answer to prayer. Even a lady who lives in California was healed of cancer. Nothing is too hard for God. We prayed here in my kitchen with some ladies from our prayer group and we laid hands on one of us in proxy for the lady in California. Much later, the lady flew to Vancouver to meet the ladies who prayed, as we were the only ones who had prayed for her. She had a large cancer in her tummy and within days of the prayer, the cancer was totally gone. She joyously shared all this as she thanked us.

18

THE ETERNITY CLUB

IN OCTOBER 1979, THE ETERNITY CLUB, AN OUTREACH MINISTRY to reach my neighbourhood for Christ, began. It was held in a small community center behind my home. This resulted from a vision the Lord gave me in the spring of 1979. After about six months of prayer, we began with only five people coming at first. Now we have as many as fifty-three coming. We meet weekly on Monday nights for prayer, praise, speaking the Word of God, and fellowship, followed by the serving of refreshments.

I knew this was of God, because on our first gathering we prayed and asked the Lord if this club was what He wanted, that He would please supply pamphlets to advertise—one hundred in all—and live music for this venture. Within a week, Kingsway Foursquare, my home church, supplied the pamphlets and a Christian band, "The Joyful Sound," offered their services for a month for free. Wow! This really was what God wanted! Many of the one hundred led to Christ were born again at this club. Young people who were heavy into excessive booze, partying, and drugs, have received Christ and turned their backs on evil and are following Jesus as dynamic witnesses for Him. The club members are now leading souls to Christ. What a joy to see Christians growing in grace!

This is awesome but true and written from my heart. Growing in grace has taken me to a place where my happiness is not based on people, things, or circumstances, but on the facts as they are written in the Bible. I am surely a pilgrim here on earth. My real home is in Heaven, where my heart is. For the joy set before me to live eternally with my Lord Jesus, I patiently endure all things. I have ecstatic joy at times and tribulation at other times, but my times are in my Lord's hands. I endure down here in His strength, not mine, for He said in Philippians 4:13 that I can endure all things through Christ which strengthens me. God is really true, otherwise how could all of these wonderful things be happening? How could I have such deep peace and strength even when it appeared my world was coming apart and my home repeatedly being broken up? It sure is true! I have received power since the Holy Ghost has come upon me (Acts 1:8).

Another wonderful thing I experience is that power now reaches to my feeling level. I actually feel His power; however, there is a time when God tries you and you do not feel His strength or presence. He is teaching us the faith walk. Faith pleases God. Jesus Christ is the author and finisher of our faith. This knowledge has comforted me so very much, because since He is the author and finisher of my faith, I can rest in His care. He does all things well.

The "glory to God" existence that I now have is a result of having come through the trials I have had, and the Lord has blessed me with the faith to believe for victory, no matter how I felt. Now I feel His presence almost all the time. As this is being written, joy floods my soul because God is no respecter of persons. What He has done for me, He wants to and is willing to do for everyone—especially YOU, dear reader.

Oh, what joy to have given your life—such as it may be—to Christ that you may have new life, abundantly in His grace, strength, and love. All through this faith walk and living I have been willing to work in the secular world at a regular job. I believe, however, that God has called me and ordained me to do the work of an evangelist, speaking and leading many precious people to Christ, through exercising the gift of evangelism. In answer to fervent prayers, doors are opening for me to speak. One of the biggest ones is the Eternity Club. I will enlarge on the opened doors in later chapters.

19

DREAMS AND
MORE DREAMS

FOR TWO NIGHTS IN A ROW I HAD INTERESTING DREAMS. IN ONE I was in a classroom with a teacher who said to me, "You have been renewed in the spirit of your mind."

"Yes, I know," I replied. "I've been reading God's Word and absorbing it into my mind."

Upon awakening, I prayed to understand this dream, and the answer came. The Lord was encouraging me that my mind is renewed. Praise God!

In the other dream I was cleaning and sweeping a road very diligently. After prayer, it came to me that we don't work and work and work to earn our way to Heaven. Jesus Christ obtained our gift of eternal life by grace on the cross, and it is ours for the receiving. Further, Isaiah 35:8 tells us that the Lord desires us to walk on a holy highway, and our Lord Jesus prepares the way. His Holy Spirit leads us and God the Father is our back up.

In March 1980, my eldest son, dear Ralph, a strapping, handsome blond haired and blue eyed, almost six foot lad, had come home for three days on a business trip. Seeing him was so very delightful. He was and still is at this writing, manager of a finance company. As I wrote earlier, he received Christ during this visit. I will explain here just how it came about.

On March 1, 1980, in the morning before work, Ralph and I talked about the plan of salvation while he was drinking his coffee.

"I would pray now, Mom," he said, "but I'm almost late for work. I will pray with you before I go back to Victoria."

I was so very delighted, but prayed diligently that nothing would change his mind. The next morning I asked him simply, "Are you ready to pray, Son?"

"I sure am, Mom," Ralph said.

What sweet words for a mother to hear! God is so very good! The most marvelous thing happened after this born again experience. Confidentially, I knew in my heart it would. Ralph and Marcia had been going together for about six years. They had been engaged about one year. Marcia, a tall, lovely brunette, longed to be married—especially since she had become born again. We had prayed about this. Ralph kept putting off wedding plans, but within four weeks of receiving Christ, he phoned me long distance and said, "Mom, would you like to come to a wedding?" I swallowed hard and asked him whose wedding. Ralph laughed and replied, "Mine and Marcia's."

Oh, how happy I was! The first wedding of one of my own children! They were married on a very beautiful spring day in Victoria. Monique, Davie, Evelyn, and I attended. It was a small but lovely wedding, with the reception in Ralph and Marcia's two bedroom home. They are blessed to be within walking distance of a lovely beach. At this writing, I am expecting something similar to happen with my son David, who is now twenty years old. He is born again, and God will supply him with a partner of His choice.

After being married four times, widowed once, divorced twice, and at this moment separated from Jim, I'm not concerning myself, for my life belongs to God, purchased by the precious blood of my Lord Jesus. My times continue to be in God's mighty hand. I know the importance of being married in the will of God. Life will always have its ups and downs, and surely we need to be where God wants us to be—in the centre of His will, which is where we will be the most happy. The Bible says doing the will of God is a delightful thing. Once we are yielded to Him, He works in us to will and do of His pleasure, and we will enjoy doing what God wants us to do, even if it is a bit difficult at times, because when we are in the centre of God's will, we are in line with His blessings and strength.

The day Ralph asked Jesus to be Lord was one of the best days of my life. I sure was on the go, though. In the morning, Ralph became born again. In that afternoon, two young brothers needed counselling and prayer. Then, I lost my little address book that was very important to me. After prayer, it was found. In the evening, I went to Women Aglow at the Hotel Vancouver with Anna H., a dear sister in Christ with whom I'm very close. It was heavenly. We sang praises to our Lord, had prayer, and heard a powerful speaker.

Coming home I was weary, but no sooner was my car parked when the phone rang. It was Michelle B., a college chum from when I lived in Campbell River. She was in town for one night and had her two sisters with her from Quebec. Michelle asked me to go and pick them up. I was so tired, and she was all the way downtown—about seven miles away. I went in Christ's love. Did God ever honour my good deed of picking them up and offering my home for them to sleep in! All the way driving back home I was sharing the love of Jesus. I was telling them the Good News, and they were all ears. They barely understood English, so Michelle, who could speak English fluently, was interpreting.

After we were back in my little kitchen sitting on my colonial chairs, we enjoyed a hot drink. The time was right to ask them if they would like to ask Jesus Christ into their lives to be Lord and Saviour. Michelle interpreted and they both said exuberantly, "Oui, oui!" My heart was so glad, and I no longer felt tired. We joined hands and through our interpreter, Jeannette and Helen became born again Christians. What an awesome delight to Michelle and I, who had received Christ during our college days. These dear French sisters in Christ both had tears of joy flowing down their cheeks. Wow! A day of days: two people led to receive Jesus, and one a family member. Praise the Lord!

In my notes, in March 1980, it is written: "Thou art holy, Thou art worthy, and Thou art mine". These precious words came to me while I was quite ill and resting. As I wrote before, they come back to comfort me. I phoned a Christian pastor, Ken Blue, and shared the words. He encouraged my heart by telling me that this was from the Lord. I now realize that any holiness or worthiness is through Jesus Christ, and we who are born again belong to Jesus, bought and paid for by His precious blood. It thrills my heart to know that Jesus considers me as "Thou art Mine." Many times while driving I've broken into a giggle. It's a good thing I've been alone in the car, as the thought has come to me repeatedly—*you have not seen anything yet, only the tip of the iceberg*—meaning much more is to follow in my walk with God. Wow!

On March 25, 1980, Michael Mooney, my sister's boy who no one wanted to even enter their house, came to my home to live. He had been in trouble since he was about seven years old. Mike was now sixteen. He had a history of breaking and entering, theft, purse snatching, car stealing, and even forging his father's signature while attempting to draw money out of his father's account at the bank. Also, he had stolen several hundred dollars from his grandmother's house. He also stole my daughter's car and wrecked it. His mother's car was also wrecked by him. On and on the life of crime went. Taking him in was quite a venture. I fully believed God could straighten out Mike's life.

On March 25, 1980, the same day as he had come to my home, he had gone to court on three charges. I prayed for him to receive mercy. Two charges were dismissed and one was suspended. Praise God for His mercy! Michael received Jesus as Lord, and he was trying to be good. However, old habits can be hard to break. Mike was willing, but he really had a bad habit of crime.

What a joy when Mike received the baptism of the Holy Spirit and was baptized in water at Kingsway Foursquare Church in Burnaby, B.C. Monique and I watched joyfully. I spoke to a judge at Family Court about Michael's progress.

"I've heard good reports of you Christians ministering to the youth," he said. "I see the results and cannot deny the progress. You may get swamped. It must be because you may have the whole church behind you." Praise God, even judges are seeing the work of our Lord Jesus through His people.

As real evidence of a keener conscience in Mike, especially after he prayed for a new heart, he said to me, "Aunt Audrey, don't pray for me to get off any charges, because I want to be punished to learn a lesson."

Around this time I received a phone call from a brother in the Lord, declaring his home situation was in an awful state. He felt his marriage of over twenty-five years was breaking up, and he asked me to phone his wife.

"For goodness sake," he said, "don't offer to pray or she will get angry."

I told him I would pray first, and I would want freedom to do and say what the Lord led me to. He told me that would be okay, because they were separated. I called, and after a lengthy conversation, we prayed and she asked Jesus to be her Lord. By faith He is, for the Bible says you cannot confess Jesus as Lord except by the Holy Ghost.

My beloved daughter, Monique, and I continued to grow in grace and were very close to each other. Her witness is different than mine. She has a gentler, quieter spirit—the same spirit that pleased God in holy women in days past. She wins souls to Christ in a gentle, sweet way. Her hair is very blonde and thick, way down past her waist. She is beautiful with the beauty of holiness, and when she walks into a room, people notice her. I am thrilled with God's work in her.

About this same time, my nephew, George Mooney, Michael's brother, came to live with us. This home was getting full! What joy to have George around. He is nineteen now, and a very good looking fellow. He attracts girls, and they are being led to Christ. I can think of two in the last two months—Angie and Kim. George loves our Lord Jesus. He is born again and was mightily touched by God at the "Jesus Fair" in Puyallup, near Portland, U.S.A. He came home filled with God's love and Holy Spirit. I know God has big plans for George. I look back now to see how my life has changed, how I no longer have a drinking or gambling problem, or a husband at home, but young people filling my house. This home is dedicated totally to my Lord, and people who come here are drawing close to God as they see Monique and my example. We have the joy of encouraging those who live and come here. There is peace, love, and joy in this home. Praise God!

Jim's departing of his own free will was God's doing, and I would like to insert that perhaps this is rare, for God's work is to save marriages, not break them up. But I know this was best for us at this time. How do I know this? Because our Lord said in His Word that cannot lie, that all things will work together for good for those that are called and love Him. I know I am called, and Jim left, so it is going to work out for the good, eventually. Bear in mind, at this writing, I know not the future. I only know my work is of God, and no man can hinder it Acts 5:38, 39).

On October 30, 1980, it was quickened to me from Revelation 3:8 that God has opened a door for me that no man can shut. Oh, how blessed this is to me, for many times I have gone out to minister God's holy Word and felt so weak, but God has honoured my faithfulness and has given me strength. I know things will get better.

20

MORE ABOUT
THE ETERNITY CLUB

I WOULD LIKE TO SHARE HOW THE ETERNITY CLUB GOT started. There is a community centre behind my home that I can see from my front room's sliding glass doors. When I would glance at it I would think that something should be done in that building for my Lord. Over and over I would think this same thought. Speaking to Monique and her friends, Eva G. and Nanette R., I asked if maybe a club for young people could be formed. Perhaps we could sing, praise God, and pray. They were very interested, so I asked them to pray about it and they did.

In the spring of 1979, I also asked Dan H., youth pastor at Kingsway, and his dear wife, Jean, to pray and ask that if it was of God, He would help keep the thought strong and alive. By October 1980, we had prayed enough and believed it was of the Lord, and it sure was. One year later we had more than forty people coming. Folks were getting saved regularly—as many as six in one night. Folks were continually being filled with the Holy Spirit and being healed. I was so very happy to be in the Lord's work, and the Lord was working with me and signs and wonders were following. The atmosphere at the hall had changed. I remember one day as

I looked out my window I saw teenagers arm in arm singing God's praises as they walked down the street.

The Eternity Club is based on Romans 6:23, "*...the gift of God is life eternal through Christ our Lord.*" Also at that time, a dear sister named Sandy C. was expecting her second child, dear Ryan, and her husband, Alf, said to her, "Since you are expecting, I guess I had better join in your "eternity club," meaning he would like to be born again. This stuck in my heart, and with the scripture promise made it a perfect name for my Lord's club.

Do you remember my prayer at New Year's? Well, God opened doors for me to speak for him. In answer to prayer, I spoke to Kingsway Foursquare Youth and at Cliff Avenue United Church, Women Aglow, Vancouver Chapter, and CJOR Radio. The greatest answer of all came on January 26, 1982, when I spoke as a guest on the *100 Huntley Street* television program.

Next to being born again, filled with the Holy Spirit, baptized in water by immersion and leading souls to Christ, the greatest knowledge God has given me is a powerful message of scriptural victory over the flesh—the old nature, who we were before we became a child of God. This victory over our sin nature is so dynamic that I share it with great joy to anyone who will hear it.

On May 6, 1980, I talked for hours with Barry M., head pastor at Kingsway Foursquare, and he confirmed that all the notes and things I shared with him were from the Lord and that truly God was speaking to me. He invited me to speak on his regular Sunday night 10:00 pm radio show, *Living Letters Program*, on CJOR. It was Mother's Day when I spoke and gave my testimony. Thanks to my Lord for answering my prayer for open doors. Barry M. and Dan H. both confirmed the Lord's call for me to do the work of an evangelist, and everywhere I go, souls are won to Christ.

21

CAMP TIMBERLINE

IN THE SUMMER OF 1980, MONIQUE AND I WENT TO CAMP Timberline in Haney (now Maple Ridge, B.C., Canada) as counsellors at an all girls' camp. There were seven girls in my cabin, of which only two were saved. In Monique's cabin there were nine girls, all of whom were unsaved. It was pretty rough for her. She had only just turned sixteen, and these girls were pretty active.

For the first few days I spent hours in prayer, claiming the whole camp for Christ. Doreen F., our capable camp director and a sister in Christ, asked Monique and me to come to camp. There was chapel every morning, but some of these girls seemed impossible to reach. However, nothing is impossible for Christ my Lord! We arrived on Sunday, and on Wednesday night things started happening.

That night while I was in the washroom the Lord quickened to me, "I've prepared her heart to receive me." I looked around and in walked a girl.

"Are you ready to ask Jesus to be your Lord?" I asked. She said that she was. We prayed, and right there she was born again.

That same night, Monique came to me and said, "Mom, a few girls in my cabin want prayer to receive Christ." And then, bless her heart, she said, "Why don't you come and pray for them and talk to my whole cabin?" It seemed right, so I did.

Well, what happened was a miracle! I simply told them the plan of salvation as they were all around, all nine of them in their bunks listening intently. Then I said, "Any of you girls who would like to pray to be born again, please come forward," and I sat down with Monique, Indian style on the floor, and the whole cabin came in a wonderful circle to receive Jesus as Lord. How our hearts rejoiced—all eleven of us! The young girls were leaping for joy and ran out into the yard, exclaiming, "I'm born again!" Praise the Lord!

I reported this event to the other Christian counsellors. I particularly befriended a gal, Ann, who had a sweet, gentle nature. One day when we drove together to a Christian book store, merrily chatting about the blessing in Monique's cabin, Ann said, "I can't even talk to my girls about spiritual things. Four of them, in particular, are going to a church where they don't believe in sin or negative thinking or talking. They believe the good in the Bible and chuck out the bad."

"Well, Ann," I said, "all things are possible with God." We prayed and agreed according to Matthew 18:19 that the same thing that happened in Monique's cabin would happen in Ann's. Then we both giggled. It was such a big prayer of faith. Led by the Holy Spirit over the next day and a half, I befriended these four girls Ann discovered one of them had a headache for over a day. I'm sure it was causing grief to that dear girl, so I said, "Can I pray to God to remove your headache?"

"You sure can! Right now, okay?" she said.

We went into her cabin and the other three gals followed. I prayed specifically, taking authority in Jesus' name over this evil headache, to acknowledge the presence of evil in the world to these four. Then I bound it and commanded it to go and asked God to heal her. I also cast off, in Jesus' name, all works of darkness from all four of those dear girls, and loosed the power of God's Holy Spirit upon them.

A little later she came to me and said that God had healed her headache. I immediately asked her if she desired to receive Jesus Christ as Lord.

"Oh, yes, I do, and so do my friends. Can they too, please?" she answered.

Well, I was thrilled! All four wanted to receive Christ. Hallelujah! It was dinner bell time, so we had to wait until after dinner. I told her I would meet them in their cabin after dinner. Lo and behold, when I went to their cabin, all the girls were there—about eight of them. Dear Ann came with me. Instinctively, I knew to share the words of life, similar to what I had done in Monique's cabin, and a second miracle happened. Ann's whole tough cabin came to Christ with tears of joy in their eyes. God was really moving and saving people. He still is.

Another miracle occurred while I was driving along, close to Champlain Mall, about six blocks from home. I desired a cup of coffee (in those days I still drank coffee). I went to Ricky's Pancake House and saw a sad looking man sitting by himself. He actually had a hound dog expression on his face. I cheerfully went to sit at the table next to him. We began to talk, and I quickly got around to my favourite subject, the Lord Jesus. He was extremely interested. I did not stop at sharing the plan of salvation, but went on to the baptism of the Holy Spirit. He said that he would like to have all these blessings that I had shared with him. So, right there in the restaurant, we prayed together and he became born again and received the baptism of the Holy Spirit from my Lord Jesus.

"If you knew who I am, you probably would not have been talking to me of all these things," he said when we had finished praying.

I wondered who he was. Perhaps he was the mayor!

"I'm an Orthodox priest," he said.

Well, we have an Orthodox priest in the city of Vancouver who is born again and filled with the Holy Spirit.

CHAPTER 22

JIM'S BACK HOME AGAIN

For my brother, Leonard's, birthday, dear Terry, his wife, threw a gala party. There was good food, music, and lots of family members. To my utter amazement, Jim walked in with Bud P., my brother-in-law. They were both inebriated. Every person stopped talking and started wondering what would happen since these two potential trouble makers had arrived. It certainly was not unusual for a fellow that was drunk to make a scene. Well, to our relief, they both coped quite well. I spent most of my time in the kitchen area, encouraging Jim to drink coffee. Rarely had I seen Jim so very obliging and sweet and gentle. He captured my heart, telling me that he had never seen me look more beautiful. Bear in mind, he had been gone from home for ten months, and I had been coping extremely well in the Lord's strength, but somehow with him being so kind, I longed immediately for him to return home.

Jim talked a bit with Evelyn, now twenty-five, and asked her to coax me into giving him an opportunity to come home. I wanted to say "yes," but I knew that I should pray and also seek wise counsel. Seeking advice, one man of God said, "You really can't refuse to forgive or try to make a home together." Another man of God encouraged deep caution, as taking him home too soon could be damaging to the wonderful walk I now enjoyed with the Lord. Jim looked so rough and pathetically lonely, and it felt good to be needed.

To this day, I'm not sure that it was a wise move. I was moved with compassion, however, so Jim came home. He promised to go to AA and also to Burden Bearers, a really good counselling service that gets to the root of problems. I was really excited about his commitment to go to Burden Bearers, knowing full well the drinking was only an outcome of a root problem, a root reason. But Jim never went to Burden Bearers. Things were not too bad for several months, but then they began to deteriorate very quickly.

Trying to quit drinking in his own strength was, and still is, impossible for Jim. He really tried. I know he did, but the outcome was inevitable as long as he was not allowing Jesus to be Lord. Jesus was in Jim's heart because he asked Him in, but our Lord never overrides our will. If we don't allow Him Lordship of our lives so that we can cope in His strength and have peace no matter what is happening, He will not exercise Lordship. We thus give place to evil and have all kinds of problems. Jim was not yielded to the Lordship of Jesus Christ. He would not let God be God so that his life would be in order with a loving Father guiding him into the way to live that was best for him. I tried in the Lord's love to encourage Jim to yield to Christ as Lord, but whenever I talked about the Lord, Jim considered it preaching. Even telling him of an answer to prayer was considered preaching. It was like trying to box with my hands tied behind my back to stay quiet about my Lord, but I tried. Oh, how I tried—especially when Jim yelled! I prayed for God to slow him down. I realize that Jim was under heavy conviction, due to my close walk with God, and he was drawing away. This truly caused him to feel guilty, and the natural response to that is irritability.

The situation reached a peak on June 25, 1981, when Jim once again left me. This time I told him three times, twice when he was sober, "If you persist in leaving me again, you will not be able to come back unless you will have already gone to Burden Bearers and also AA." My reasoning was that this ultimatum would eventually cause Jim to seek help. At this writing, Jim has been gone for three months, and again God has marvelously supplied my needs and those of my daughter Monique and my daughter Lily, who has been home for months with my new grandson, little Miles. Lily allowed me to come into the delivery room and I witnessed a natural birth. Praise God for His creation—us!

One day at the Eternity Club, a dear gal came to me and said, "The Lord directed me to give you this." With tears in her eyes, she pressed a one hundred dollar cheque into my hand. The ministry God has called me to be His, and He is supplying all my needs, exceedingly, abundantly, above all I could ask or think. I am still believing God for total deliverance for Jim. I am doing the believing and leaving all the results and the timing up to God Almighty. I am continuing to thank God that I married an alcoholic, because through it all I am learning to trust in Jesus. I am learning to trust in God. The joy and peace I have now is so very wonderful and beyond words. I thank my Lord for Christian friends like Garret G. who loves Jesus with all his heart as he assists me in the ministry and encourages me in finishing this book.

I also thank God for precious people like Mike and Janus M., who minister in music at the Club and in friendship. Most special is Doreen H., who has been my counsellor. Doreen knew all along, as I did in my heart, that God placed a mighty call on my heart and life. I respond to that call with an awesome love and eagerness, never losing the thrill to pray with someone to receive Jesus as Lord. Thank God for

Dave Z., David L., and Rob F., who are faithful to the Eternity Club. In my first year and a half working as an evangelist, almost two hundred folks received Christ, and close to fifty had prayer for the baptism of the Holy Spirit and the manifestation of speaking in tongues. People continue to be healed. At one point, Rheal C., Monique's natural father, was healed of a serious blood pressure condition.

The greatest joy, next to leading souls to Christ, is that Monique works at my side in this precious ministry of our Lord Jesus. Monique had several months of giving into temptation and turning away from Christ, but it did not take long for an answer to prayer. Monique quickly came back to Jesus.

In life on this earth there always will be problems, but in Christ's strength these very problems can be stepping stones to strength. As long as we run to Jesus Christ for help, as I have in my troubled times, especially with Jim's drinking problem, we will find help. When you know Jesus Christ and you have trials and tribulations, they will work patience and trust in you, and these will truly be stepping stones to strength. God has clearly shown me He is building an "army" of people who will be strong—not wishy-washy milk sops—but strong people who will not fall apart as world conditions deteriorate. They will be strong people, in Jesus Christ's strength, who can walk on water, go through trials and tribulations, and keep their eyes on Jesus, the author and finisher of their faith. I enclose a prayer that the Lord quickened to me that said faith will give you the victorious life, victory over the world, the devil and the flesh, which is the old nature we were before Christ came into our lives and we inherited His nature, infused into us. May the Lord work with you, and may signs and wonders be following you as Christ is glorified in you, dear reader, is my prayer.

This prayer is for born-again believers. A powerful victory prayer said daily, mixed with faith, can scripturally help give victory over the flesh, the world and the devil!

Heavenly Father, I deny myself, pick up my cross and follow Jesus Christ, my Lord. I yield myself to do God's will, to be led by the Holy Spirit. I am crucified to this world, and this world is crucified to me by the cross of my Lord Jesus. The old man is nailed to the cross of my Lord Jesus, and I forbid him to come off, in Jesus' name. I reckon myself indeed dead to sin, to the power of sin, guilt, and the old man, and alive unto God through Jesus Christ. I am not conformed to this world, but transformed by the renewing of my mind, having put on the new man, created in righteousness and true holiness. Fill me afresh with Your Holy Spirit and strength to walk in the spirit of Jesus Christ, my Lord. I submit to You, resist satan, and cast off all works of darkness in Jesus' name. I plead the blood of Jesus Christ over me and my family. I put on the whole armour of God and go forth victorious.

I pray and say this in Jesus Christ's mighty name, for Your honour and glory, Lord. Amen.

Scripture promises that are in the above powerful prayer:

Luke 9:23	Romans 6:6	Ephesians 5:18
Romans 8:14	Romans 6:11	Ephesians 4:24
Romans 12:1 - 2	Galatians 6:14	Ephesians 6:11
Romans 13:12	Galatians 5:16 – 18	James 4:7
Revelation 12:11		

Dear reader, if you do not as yet know Jesus Christ as your personal Lord and Saviour and desire to, please pray this simple, but powerful and meaningful prayer:

Father, I believe Jesus died on the cross and God raised Him from the dead. I confess I have sinned and I am sorry, Lord. I ask Jesus Christ to come into my life and be my personal Lord and Saviour. Jesus Christ is my Lord. Amen

If you have prayed this prayer, please contact the ministry and we will do our best to send you a free gift to help you walk with God, through Christ our Lord. Amen.

www.eternityclub.org
www.audreymabley.org
604-437-5500

BEGINNING OF THE ETERNITY CLUB MINISTRY— HOW GOD CAN BEGIN A MINISTRY!

In 1979, while Audrey Mabley was just a young Christian, she only had a personal relationship with Christ as Lord for a few years. One evening, as she was closing the sliding door curtains in the co-op where she lives, she heard the voice of Jesus say to her

"Shouldn't something be happening in there for me?" She glanced outside and saw the Kanata Community Hall behind her home, and she knew the Lord meant for her to begin something for Him in this hall.

So, she began to pray and think, what would be good to do for the Lord? Recalling how she had been very blessed at Aglow Meetings, she thought to start something like that, with music, worship and sharing in God's word, and prayer for needs. Her youngest daughter, Monique, was a teenager and Audrey asked her if she started some meetings would she come and invite her friends? Monique said she would.

So, they had a planning meeting. Her daughter, Monique, her neighbour, Sandy, and herself. They talked about what to name the ministry. Recalling that Sandy's husband had said to her when she was expecting his baby, "since you're having my baby, I'd better join your Eternity Club," meaning to become a Christian, it was agreed that would be the name and it still is today.

Sometime later, she again heard the Lord say to her thoughts *"founder of the Eternity Club."* She knew instantly the Lord meant it would be a good work and a large work. Joy flooded her soul. Once again praying, she asked the Lord to supply live music, food to follow the first meeting and pamphlets to advertise it. The church she was attending offered to print pamphlets at no cost, a band named Joyful Sound offered to do worship and a catering company provided food (lots of it). That was the first meeting and God put His Seal of Blessing on it!

In the beginning, mainly teenagers came, friends of Audrey's daughter, who she had invited from school, and young neighbour kids. So, there were 30 – 50 regulars coming to the Club.

One Monday night, Mike M. came in on crutches with a pulled ligament in his knee. They prayed for him, laid hands on him and he was healed! Three days later, Audrey saw him skateboarding. This was the beginning of regular healings. Young people were coming to Christ and the hall that was a hangout for teenagers to drink and be rowdy was now a place of prayer and worship. One day, Audrey looked out her kitchen window and she saw 3 or 4 teenagers arm in arm dancing and singing about Jesus! Tears come to her eyes as she recalls this blessing.

As the years went by, people who lived in Kanata started complaining because their young people were becoming Christians and they were of another faith. So they began a work to make it so that The Eternity Club couldn't meet at the hall. They were, finally, successful but, Praise God, Kingsway Four Square Church knew of her need and offered a meeting place for the Eternity Club. They also put her on staff and gave her credentials as a Reverend. They saw clearly that Audrey was called to be an Evangelist. Her converts were coming to church and being water baptised there. Soon, they gave her an office, free printing and a small housing allowance. Having all this provided, enabled her to expand beyond Monday night meetings. Film night and Daniel's Den Coffee House were added outreach ministries. At every event, the Gospel was given and people came to Christ.

In the spring of 1989, the church leadership informed Audrey that their support had come to an end because they believed that she should continue to pursue her original mandate to be inter-denominational. This caused extreme distress for Audrey, tears and sadness such as she had rarely known in her life. But, on her knees praying to Jesus, He spoke to her telling her to have hope and faith and He would bring her through this sad time. She committed everything to the Lord again, including her life and future. She said to Him, from the depths of her heart "If I never lead another person to Christ or see another healing, I shall be eternally grateful for all You've done through my life these 20 years of serving You." Great peace enveloped her as God took the burden.

She began to pray earnestly with others that more than fifteen needs would be provided so the Ministry could carry on and this would be confirmation God desired it to continue. She didn't make it easy for the Lord, on the list was a van for people to be picked up for meetings (before, the church had provided a van). Other things on the list were a sound system and a place to meet, and every single need came in.

Now, having her own facility, she began a food bank and weekly drop in centres for people to come and have a snack, fresh coffee, and enjoy Christian Fellowship. The Ministry was having events five to six times a week. They were, Tuesday, Wednesday and Thursday, drop in centre; food bank once a week, Friday night Daniel's Den Coffee House, Sunday service with full meals – spaghetti, chilli, lasagne – always enough for at least forty people to eat; and once a month Saturday night film night. Audrey and her team were soaring for Jesus.

Barbara Hill
Reverend Audrey Mabley's Secretary
August 7, 2014

THIRTY-PLUS YEARS
LATER UPDATE

Through perseverance, love, and faith, we win out.

Beloved reader, it has been over thirty years since I took pen and paper to write my true life story. I felt in my heart it would be good to write an update.

I'm sitting in my kitchen, having just finished a good cup of tea, still living in our humble co-op in Vancouver, reflecting on how things are and the awesome God given changes that have taken place. I am now seventy-five years old and in basic good health. At present, I'm doing nation-wide television and radio and involved in church planting. For over a dozen years we ran "Daniel's Den Coffee House," an alternative to neighbourhood pubs, where there was live music, a mini café, and rich fellowship. Some who met there ended up getting married. At present time, and for about ten years, every fall and spring we have revival healing services and see many miracles.

When you consider my past, this is nothing short of amazing. Truly, God can use any willing, yielded vessel. I have witnessed multiple healings personally and in others in answer to prayer. Lives changed, deliverances, people set free from alcohol and other problems! I am totally convinced there is nothing too hard or impossible for God Almighty.

He is greater than any need we will ever have or hear about. I challenge you to believe this with me. Amen!

The longest Jim was away was a year and a half. During that time, I realized some of my maturing as an adult was stuck at age fifteen, which is when I got married. I thought I couldn't live without a man in my life telling me what to do. I believe this was because my dad had ruled our home and Mom did every single thing he said, and that rubbed off on me. Now I discovered I could live without a man in my life. This brought me great confidence and liberty. From the time I was fifteen, there had been a man in my life, so now I matured more as a grown up Christian lady.

The local church I attended had taken me on staff as an Eternity Club coordinator with a housing allowance of six hundred dollars. That was the start of God providing two thousand dollars each month. Hallelujah! God answers prayers indeed.

Jim's coming and going occurred over a span of about ten years. After that, he was keeping in touch with my daughters and buying all the disposable diapers when they had babies. When Lily lived in the same co-op as me, I would see Jim going over to her house as he walked past my home. I wondered if it could be God's will for us to try one more time for our marriage to work. I sought Godly counsel from ministers who I trusted and respected. They are well known in my area. A few said that taking Jim back would be like having a dead man to carry on my back. That sounded horrible, of course. One said he likely would get sick (from the alcohol I suppose), and I could spend my energy taking care of him and have no time for God's work. Another few said God is glorified by a healed marriage. I was so confused. I got down on my knees on the hard floor where I am now writing (I have a tear welling up as I remember). I was longing "only" to please God and do His will. It seemed to me the nudging from God was to see if Jim even wanted to come home.

I finally decided to call Jim to ask him if he wanted to work on our marriage. He was at my door within ten minutes and never left again.

He came home a sober man. He has been sober ever since, over twenty-five years now. Once a person is an alcoholic, however, even when they quit drinking there is still reasons in their life why they turned to alcohol. Those reasons made it so that it was still not an easy road to a blessed, Christ honouring marriage. I was "on fire for God," but he was not.

I expected great change; after all, he was sober and he had asked Jesus into his life. I think he expected great changes, too. I think (my thoughts only, God knows the reality of what happened) a lot of people ask Jesus into their hearts to escape Hell, but they may not really want Jesus to be Lord/Master of their life. God knows, not me, who is sincere when they come to Christ. There were some changes, for sure. When Jim was working in Kamloops, B.C. he went to church. He was even reading the Bible, but something he read troubled him, and to my knowledge he has never picked it up again, nor has he attended church for about twenty years.

It appears as though some get their foot in Heaven's door, but don't have a lot of Heaven in them because of lack of growth. Have you ever met a confessing Christian who doesn't act much different than people of the world? Most likely they are not in God's Word, which is our spiritual food that helps us grow spiritually into Christ likeness: "*Desire the sincere milk of the word, that ye may grow thereby*" (1Peter 2:2).

Being very truthful, we do have a miracle marriage, mainly because often it's like we live in two different worlds, but Jim doesn't try to stop me from serving God. When he came home, I told him that if I perceived something was of

God, I would do it—period. He has accepted that, so I sing to the Lord in our home (mostly in my bedroom), I read God's Word, and carry on as a "soldier of Christ." Jim does what he pleases, pretty well, but there are no "R" rated shows or nudity on TV in our house. He likes police shows. I mainly like old westerns and comedies. Like they say, men are from Mars and women from Venus! The only way, in my humble opinion, for a couple to really become like minded is if they both yield to Christ as Lord and follow Him together. That always is my hope and prayer.

In 1990 I came into some money, so I asked Jim what it would take for him to quit smoking.

"Take me on a cruise," he answered.

"I will, but you need to quit for a full year," I said. You see, he had quit twice before, but after seven months started smoking again.

He did quit. No more smoke smelling bedroom, car port, or house! But he sure was grumpy! He acted ornery and "out of sorts." There are lots of levels of that, and they can hurt. By God's grace, I try always to give a "gentle word" that turns away wrath (Proverbs 15:1). If I render "nastiness" back to Jim, It's never long before I repent to God and ask for forgiveness from Jim. You see, we are not to render evil for evil (1 Peter 3:9). It's important when we are hurt to pray for healing. Christ the Lord "heals" even broken hearts. Thank God!

Honestly, I have needed many healings. I look at my husband as a diamond in the rough, and he is God's workmanship, not mine. I must not try to be his mother. Do I ever do that? More than I'd like to admit.

In our co-op, Jim is some kind of "hero," as he works year after year (over twelve now) as a volunteer up to twenty or thirty hours per week, helping out folks. That is the diamond shining through. He likes to cook meals (too often for my liking at times, as it can put on weight), and he even does all the shopping.

We go to Starbucks together at times, and I really like their hot chocolate. Jim likes their apple fritters. Eating breakfast out together with Monique is a peaceful blessing time we both enjoy weekly. Thank God we can afford it. Many seniors cannot.

As for my walk with God, the Foursquare Church welcomed me on staff, and for twelve years God enabled me to oversee and lead Daniel's Den Coffee House Ministry, film nights, and Monday night Eternity Club meetings, where we regularly saw healing, miracles, and above all, salvations. However, the leadership decided I should pursue my original mandate and be what they call "interdenominational," meaning not under one church. It would be an "over the wall" ministry, but it meant no salary, no office, and no meeting place. I almost fell apart! I was so concerned about the ministry that God began through my life. I was so downcast.

I went up to my bedroom to pray. It was Mother's Day, and Jim told the girls who had come to visit me to leave me alone, as I was having a hard time. I got down on my knees beside my bed to pray and ask God to help me carry on and know what to do.

I felt like I was going to fall apart. While seeking God, my eyes fell to the little book on my night table titled, *A Christian's Secret of a Happy Life* by Hannah Whitall Smith. I picked it up and saw I had not read the last chapter. The first few words gave me hope. God was helping me. The words basically said if you are downcast, then one of your wings of faith and trust is down. I realized that is where I was at.

I said to God: "If I never lead another person to Christ, or the ministry does not continue, I shall be eternally grateful for all you have done through my life." Such a peace came over me as I sincerely released it all to God. I got up off my knees and went downstairs and joined my family and enjoyed my "special day."

Soon after this I put a kind of "fleece" before God, asking Him to do something to confirm (give me a sign) that He wanted me to continue in ministry. I made a list of about fifteen things we would need. I did NOT make it simple for the Lord, as on the list was a Van (to pick up folks to come to meetings), chairs, a meeting place, an office, sound equipment and a film projector for film nights, etc. Everything on the list came in! Surely God wanted me to continue in His Eternity Club ministry.

Now let me bubble over about God's greatness as He shows what He can do with a yielded vessel. The ministry evolved from coffee house, film nights, and Monday meetings to doing church planting (one English church and helping two Korean churches). Further, over ten years ago, a Christian Television program called *Eternally Yours* came into being. Presently, it is on five stations in Canada weekly and available on Internet (www.eternallyyourstv.org). For going on the second decade, we also have an M-F radio broadcast called *Mabley Moments*. Sharing God's Love and Word over the air waves is a great delight to me, as I am being God's mouthpiece (Jeremiah 15:19). What an honour and joy. To God be the praise!

Most blessed is the fruit of the "labour of love." People coming to know God loves them and through sincerely "receiving" Jesus Christ in their lives as Lord and Saviour can grow and live more and more in God's strength by the blessed Holy Spirit.

This is my life going forward (I breathe in a "restful sigh") as I enter "God's rest" (Hebrews 4:1). I daily spend quality time with God in His word, praying and quietly waiting on Him. I'm longing and having Father God reveal more and more of His love and glorious life sustaining strength and presence to me.

Now that you've read my story, please take time to think where you will spend eternity. My prayer is it will be where I am going to live forever in a glorified body, where there is no more pain, sorrow, or crying. I expect to dance with Jesus on the streets of gold. Hope to see you there one day! AMEN!

A FINAL NOTE:
PRAYERS "GALORE" ANSWERED

God hears and answers prayers—absolutely, for sure! He comes for our words like He did for Daniel in Daniel 10:12. Here are a few answers:

My husband saved, set free from alcohol.

All my offspring have confessed Jesus as Lord.

The funds came in to publish my book.

Since 1999, I have been enabled to receive a minister's salary.

My left knee received a miracle healing of a torn meniscus, and my surgery was cancelled (just one of multiple healings recorded in a booklet on my night table). Hallelujah!

I had an artery that was totally healed. My Dr. Golin said it's a miracle, because when a pipe is rusty it does not get unrusty. Amen!

My family is also doing well. Ralph, my oldest, is a successful government worker living with his dear wife, Marcia, in Victoria, B.C. They raised a lovely gal, Christina, who is married to Scott.

Evelyn married John, and has lived in New Zealand for over twenty years. She is a successful real estate agent. They have one beautiful, twenty-one year old daughter, Kathryn Joy.

David went to be with the Lord over twenty years ago. He had one daughter, Lisa, and two grandchildren.

Lily lives in a suburb of Vancouver, Maple Ridge. She raised three fine sons: Clint, Miles, and Christopher.

Jeannette, my adopted out daughter, married Frank, and raised a son and daughter, Michael and Michelle.

My youngest, Monique, raised two fine Christian lads, Kevin and Luis. They all have brought great joy to me and my seventy-eight old husband. They are always close to us, making every Christmas, birthday, and special day really wonderful. They share their lives with us old folks! Praise God!

At this date, I am blessed with thirteen grandchildren. Two are great grandchildren, and one is a great, great grandchild—Alexis is five years old.

———————————

For all of these blessings and strength to carry on for Jesus' sake, I give Him the honour and praise and lastly ask for you to please pray for me. In Jesus Christ's name and love. May God richly bless you.

Reverend Audrey Mabley

Audrey & Monique, her youngest, 1975

Last picture of Audrey, her Mom & Dad, 1989

Audrey & her four daughters at double wedding October 3, 1987
Jeannette, Monique, Audrey, Lily, & Evelyn

Audrey in her backyard, 2012

Pat Morten, patient cameraman #1

Telecast cameraman 2, Stuart Spani

Audrey & Daughter Lily Ann, 1994, Ministry 15th Celebration

Audrey at Ministry 35th Celebration

Audrey & Daughter Monique, Ministry 35th Celebration

Audrey at the 35th Celebration of Ministry

Rev. Audrey Mabley, 2013

Celebrating Audrey's 75th, 2013

Audrey & James, October 2013, at Ministry 35ᵗʰ Celebration

Six sisters: Marie, Audrey, Carole, Marion, Jeanne & Joanne, 1971

Audrey's sister Carole at her son's wedding, 1980

CPSIA information can be obtained at www.ICGtesting.com
Printed in the USA
LVOW01s0343261214

420367LV00011B/126/P